NOT OUR KIND OF FOLKS?

**DICK BROGAN,
Compiler**

Broadman Press
Nashville, Tennessee

© Copyright 1978 • Broadman Press
All rights reserved.

4255-89
ISBN: 0-8054-5589-2

Dewey Decimal Classification: 241.3
Subject heading: PREJUDICES AND ANTIPATHIES CHRISTIAN ETHICS

Library of Congress Catalog Card Number: 77-87840
Printed in the United States of America

Dedication

Dedicated to the numerous pastors, church-staff members, and lay persons in Mississippi churches who are a part of the contemporary struggle for human rights and the eradication of prejudice.

Foreword

In his inaugural address, President Carter declared, "We have already found a high degree of personal liberty, and we are now struggling to enhance equality of opportunity. Our commitment to human rights must be absolute, our laws fair, our natural beauty preserved; the powerful must not persecute the weak, and human dignity must be enhanced. . . . The world itself is now dominated by a new spirit. Peoples more numerous and more politically aware are craving and now demanding their place in the sun—not just for the benefit of their own physical condition but for basic human rights. . . . I hope that when my time as your President has ended we (will) have torn down the barriers that separated those of different race and region and religion and, where there (has) been mistrust, built unity, with a respect for diversity."

Speaking to the issue of human rights, the Southern Baptist Convention in 1977 resolved that: "We reaffirm our belief in the free exercise of religion as determined by a free conscience, and that we oppose any discrimination, legal or otherwise, against any individual based upon race, age, gender, or nationality, and that in reaffirming our opposition to such discrimination, we also express our opposition to all governmental efforts to define discrimination in such a way that ridiculous extremes, repugnant to the Christian faith and life, become the law of the land."

The contributors to this work share the conviction that prejudice must be confronted before basic human rights may be enjoyed. If "it does matter to me what happens to you," then we must face any bias that may deny you of your rights and deprive you of our gift of love. May our struggles with prejudice and basic rights probe and challenge you so that those who are not our kind of folks may become our kind of folks by the grace of God.

DICK BROGAN
Jackson, Mississippi

Contents

Not Our Kind of Folks?

1.
Prejudice Has Many Faces

James M. Porch

Life cannot be lived in a vacuum. Society cannot flourish in a closet and few of us can afford the privilege of spending time as Thoreau did in a Walden setting. Instead, we go and come day by day in a culture filled with people. We discover many of the lessons of our human existence as we run the risk of exposing ourselves to other people. In the course of our contacts with different human beings, we become vulnerable to becoming a prejudicial person. Actually, every part of life that involves relationships between human beings becomes a potential area for prejudice.

Prejudice has been a much-written-about subject during the last twenty years. Most writers addressing themselves to the problem of prejudice have recorded two admissions. That is: (1) prejudice exists; (2) we need to get rid of it.

Both of these conclusions are worthy subjects for study but they overlook another basic issue, "What are the causes for one's prejudice?"

You may build a case for the causes of your prejudice based on your present environment or the malady of your heritage. Yet, a person can, if he is honest, structure a much stronger case for the existence of personal prejudice built on his personal responsibility for his prejudicial views, for example, the prejudices he has encountered and his reaction to them.

This chapter proposes to present some of the prejudices I have encountered and my reaction to them. Here, the basic conviction is that prejudice is learned.

It is interesting, also, that much that has been written about prejudice has been limited to racial prejudice. In fact, the vast majority of Christian ethics textbooks have limited their treatment of the subject to the race issue. It has reflected the number one prejudicial issue in America. Now even though the war on race prejudice is far from victory, the Christian has a responsibility to address himself to the ever-expanding gamut of prejudice that takes its toll on all aspects of life.

The subject, "Prejudice Has Many Faces," can be approached either historically or institutionally. However, in view of my conviction concerning personal responsibility for prejudice, I have chosen to review the different prejudices I have encountered during my life. Therefore, the nature of this discussion is a confession.

The Faces of Prejudice I Have Met

I grew up in a small central Mississippi town.

My father was a town blacksmith and my mother was a housewife. I was their only child. Our home was a happy place and we loved and respected each other.

Religious Prejudice

Our family was Baptist and we lived behind the Methodist church. In our town you were either Baptist or Methodist. We had two halftime churches and we visited each one on alternate Sundays. The only religious distinction was Methodist sprinkling versus Baptist immersion and the fact that the Methodist church had a steeple.

The real religious prejudice began one day when a doctor moved to town to set up a practice. He was a Catholic and also was the only doctor in town. He was gradually accepted because of his medical knowledge, but was a social outcast because of his religion. I distinctly remember the day the word began circulating that the Catholic doctor and his family had been invited to a wedding at the Baptist church. The tension could be likened to the conditions surrounding any rumor today that a black person planned to attend the Baptist church next Sunday. This was my first experience with the manipulation of a person for what he could do and the lack of acceptance of a person for what he was. The impact of this experience was highlighted years later as I had to encounter the personhood of Catholics as I accepted a New Orleans pastorate in an area where Baptists were in the minority.

Race Prejudice

Our town was a typical Mississippi village with its own man-made segregation boundary. In the eastern part of town there was a street separating Mill Town from the white section of town. It was understood that this street separated the whites from the blacks. Black persons, it seemed to me as a child, existed for the whites. Each day blacks came over to the white area to work in trade. They served as maids, farmers, loggers, or lawnboys. At the end of the work day they returned to Mill Town.

Specifically, I remember when Uncle Andrew and Uncle Jessie came to plow for us. Their coming was preceded by taking down that special cracked china plate and special mason fruit jar from the top shelf of the cupboard. Blacks working for us always ate lunch on the back steps using those utensils. I will never forget the fateful day I asked for a fruit jar and plate so I could join Uncle Jessie. My mother told me that she would rather I eat with my father and her. I persisted and she granted my wish. In discussions with my mother since then, and knowing of her positive racial feelings now, I can better understand how the past generation succumbed to peer pressure rather than exercise personal convictions.

I cannot assess the degree of my father's racial feelings. He died in 1960, prior to our state's social change. However, I do remember that he practiced with great conviction an equality of business to each and all who came to his shop and it grieved him greatly at the way fellow businessmen took advantage of black people.

Social Prejudice

Our town's life-style differed in three basic ways from the surrounding rural area's life-style. (1) We had gas heat; the rural homes burned wood. (2) We had indoor plumbing; the rural homes had outdoor privies. (3) We walked to the nearby school; the rural children rode the tally-ho.

White and black people did many things together: we traded at the same stores; used the same roads; attended the same funerals; yet we were on two different plateaus as citizens.

There existed a strong desire and drive for community conformity to the extent that little communication existed between the various areas. The rural communities were clannish with each area having one or two families that structured life in that locale. The townspeople thought that was bad.

The depth of the division and the extent of the hard feelings surfaced in a controversy over school consolidation. The decision that was made was for the schools south of town to be closed and the children bussed to the town school. (This was 1958.) Immediately fears surfaced.

The town people were afraid that there was an education gap between town and country and that the learning process would be slowed. An inequity of cost would prevail because of the tax millage rate between town property and rural land. Finally, the town children would be subject to more diseases because country children were deprived of town sanitation.

It is surprising how happy I was ten years later in a rural pastorate.

Cultural Prejudice

During my last year in high school I went to the University of Illinois on a 4-H Club trip. This was my first jaunt outside the sovereign state of Mississippi. During the trip I saw public liquor stores, witnessed racial mixing, heard people talking funny, and could obtain no cornbread for one whole week. This was my first experience with cultural shock.

All of a sudden my little corner in east Rankin County was not representative of God's great big world. This encounter pointed up the later learned truth from Carlisle Marney that "too narrow a view of anything results in prejudice thinking and action."

Educational Prejudice

One day I went off to Mississippi College to get an education. My hometown then had very few college graduates. Furthermore, if one did receive college training he was expected to return home and practice his new skills.

I came home after one week of college convinced that I had joined the intelligentsia and now I was intellectually superior to the folks at home. It was amazing how one week on the college campus had built such a gulf between me and the citizenry of my hometown.

My father, who had a third-grade education and who had taught himself to read and write, must have known what to expect from me after one week of education. On Saturday morning, after having returned on Friday afternoon, he allowed me the privilege of cleaning up his blacksmiths shop and an adjacent hog pen. This was one of the greatest empirical lessons I have ever learned. Monday morning I returned to Mississippi College with a more realistic view of who I was.

Theological Prejudice

I began my seminary studies not really knowing what I believed. In three years I was exposed to a theological world ranging from fundamentalism to liberalism, whatever that means.

During those days our campus was the scene of a theological battle that was cruel, divisive, and vicious. Neither group trusted or respected the other. There was little communication between the camps. The result was a polarization bordering on the point of dehumanizing people, people differing from you. Belief concerning the rapture took precedence over the value and worth of the human being or even a cordial hello. That, to me, is prejudice.

Years later I encountered a second theological battle in a church I served as pastor. For one and one-half years the people in our church tried patiently to work with a small group of frustrated, semicharismatic people. During the period I personally felt that I was the main target for attack. I could say nothing from the pulpit they found satisfactory. The best way of describing the period is in the words of one of those people, "The only thing I agree with you on is the way you comb your hair." I admit I have a very strong prejudice against charismatics.

Political Prejudice

Following my city pastorate in New Orleans, I began a tenure of service in a rural area of south Mississippi. In the community there lived a patriarchal figure who had served as a county official for twenty-eight years. Also, his father had given the land for the church building. It is very difficult to assess the amount of power he possessed in the county.

I knew all graves in our beat were dug at county expense. I knew bridge timbers were used in several private buildings. I knew that private roads and driveways were being maintained by public funds. Yet I could rationalize my ethics by the fact that I believed he was doing good.

Then election time came and my wife and I were bombarded with candidates asking us to be objective. Only then did I discover that my subjectivity had led me into another area of prejudice.

Current Prejudices Being Encountered

(1) *Mass Media*—I experience frustration having

heard a major news announcement then witnessing quite different editorials by major networks as they try to tell me, "This is what he meant." This is an insult to my intelligence and makes me question the credibility and integrity of the media.

(2) *The Haves and Have Nots*—As a citizen of middle-class suburbia, I am somewhere between the haves and have-nots. I have a mortgage and I do not have several things I would like to have. My vocation is supposed to major on self-denial, but I have wants and a family that is entitled to the same comforts as any family.

(3) *Sexual*—I am involved in a vocation whose leadership has traditionally been male dominated. I think this is changing. On an average Sunday as many women as men participate in the services in our church. This has opened a new dimension of worship for me. Yet, I know what we accept and honor in our church is not the rule in other places.

(4) *Medical Prejudice*—As a pastor I come in contact almost daily with sick people. In discussion with relatives and friends of the sick, I find there are certain acceptable and certain unacceptable medical problems. For instance, it appears that many people associate weakness or the inability to cope with life to the trauma experienced by the mentally or emotionally ill person. The response is that the patient is often ignored or shunned. In addition, few churches provide an acceptable climate conducive to the healing of the sick person after he or she returns home.

(5) *Adoption Prejudice*—Among my happy roles in life is included the privilege of being a chosen

parent. We have one chosen child and as this is being written, we are awaiting the placement of our second child. In our several years as chosen parents, my wife and I have become quite sensitive to the term "illegitimate child." The use of the expression can carry the meaning that the child is of less value than normal or is the product of an unusual union. My usual response upon hearing the term is to inform the speaker that there is no such thing as an illegitimate child, rather there are only illegitimate parents.

(6) *Denominational Prejudice*—Somewhat related is the strong prejudging in the mystical, evasive, yet real, area of denominational politics.

Why can't we be realistic? A great church is often determined by its increase in warm bodies, cold cash, and whether or not the fellowship has recently constructed another brick and/or monument. On the other hand, a church in a remote area where there are few prospects for growth, limited income, and the pastor is the only staff member, can be termed a "good church." More often, it is the pastor of the "great church" that pays well to the cooperative kitty who is singled out for advancement up the denominational ladder. The religious kingmakers need to remember that the rural pastor at Route 3, who serves a congregation of fifty people, just might be more in touch with the pulse of the people than the urban pastor who struggles to keep the machinery of his administration well oiled.

Sad to say, the arena of denominational prejudice can be quite expensive, even to the point of intolerance concerning the personal identity of the local church. I suppose it was to be expected that after 130 years as a denomination, certain measuring sticks would become imposed upon a local congregation as to its success. Do we not check out a church concerning gifts to foreign missions and how many baptisms it records, even if some of these have just escaped the age of infancy? But what of the fellowship of believers, diligently struggling to relate the gospel to their everyday life pilgrimage? What about the *koinonia* that has looked upon its immediate Judea and out of deep love for humanity begins to minister to the social needs of people? Has our history imposed limited scope upon the mission of the church? If so, do we not often fear the guilt of prejudging a church according to our accepted norms for success? How inconsistent is the prejudice with our espoused denominational polity. We defend the rights of the local church to do its things, yet measure that same badly by our thing. That is prejudice.

Conclusion

I am convinced there are many other faces of prejudice that I have met. Some I have forgotten. Some I don't want to remember. Some I didn't know I was meeting. However, these I have confessed to meeting have been shared with you with a prayer that God will help us admit our prejudice so he can work in us and through us.

Having confessed to my prejudices, I must consider what can be done about my personal need for redemption. Basically, what I must hope for is continual conversion. Yes, conversion is immediate as known in the new birth encounter. However, there is a sense in which conversion is always in process. This is the work of Christ convicting me of my prejudiced spots which rob me of my potential wholeness. Once aware of these troubled parts of my being, an agony sets in as the prejudice of the hour wars with Christ's message of freedom and liberty. Sometime, somewhere, in this conflict I must make a moral decision to turn the prejudging attitude loose and experience the freedom that follows another fallen wall in my life.

2.
What Is Prejudice?

Dick Brogan

Prejudging is the activity of a prejudice carrier and all of us are infected with this "overcategorization." Applied to race, prejudice means aversion for an individual or group predicated upon inadequate knowledge. Prejudice is the illegitimate offspring of *ignorance* and *arrogance*.

"Solipsism, a theory of knowledge which says all I know is me," [1] enfleshens this perverted thought process. Prejudice refuses to gather the facts, weigh them objectively, and reach a knowledgeable position about people.

A Mental Fence

"And what is prejudice? It is a vicious kind of mental slant pushed up out of your culture that makes up your mind for you before you think. It

1. Carlyle Marney, *Structures of Prejudice* (Nashville: Abingdon Press, 1961), pp. 187, 188.

is an evil kind of mental blind spot that shuts from
your view the facts in a given situation. It is a
tyrannous mental fence that holds you from friendships you need and confines you to your own backyard. It may be racial, religious, sectional, economic,
or social. It is always personal, and in some sense
it is always cultural. It is a symptom of pride, ignorance, and ego anywhere it happens to you, and
it cuts across justice, perverts truth, subsists on lies,
and worse; it twists and wastes personality, for whose
sake culture exists to begin with." [2]

Vampire of the Mind

"And what is prejudice?" Prejudice is the vampire
of the mind, sucking dry the blood of acceptance.
Psychologist Carl Rogers noted "Acceptance on my
part is a real willingness for this other person to
be what he or she is. Acceptance says, I am willing
for this person to possess the feelings he possesses,
to hold the attitudes he holds, and to be the person
he is."

Prejudice—Opposite of Jesus

It appears to me that Jesus Christ and prejudice
are opposites. Jesus played the host role in his life.
He was vulnerable. Jesus was capable of being
wounded, liable to attack or injury, assailable, ap-

2. Carlyle Marney, *Faith in Conflict*, (Nashville: Abingdon Press, 1957), p. 87.

proachable, open. He played the host role and people were at ease in his presence. Jesus was at home with all persons. He listened to the deeper self. He was able to touch a soul with a soul. He affirmed individual personhood. He was a bridge, not a wall, in human relations. He was a window, not a mirror. He was a priest to others. Prejudice denies my being a priest. "I do not priest me," says Marney. "I priest you, and vice versa."

How Prejudice Grows

Prejudice begins its life in the seeds of segregation and separation. It grows into the stalk called lack of communication, blossoms in the rains of misunderstanding or lack of understanding, is fertilized by racial misconceptions that bear the fruit of racial stereotyping. That fruit dries, corrupts, and rots, returning to the seed of prejudice. And the cycle continues in the soil of the human heart.

Prejudice believes that it is better, cleaner, smarter, and healthier than everybody. Prejudice acts out its self-hatred, projecting that self-hatred toward others. Prejudice is dead from the top of its proud head to the bottom of its kicking foot.

When Christian love walks in the front door, prejudice runs to the back door. It doesn't leave the house. It hangs on the back screen, lingers in the shadows of selfishness, waiting for an opportunity to reenter. It continually waits to be used sending its perverted spirit into men's minds to twist and maim whole people.

Prejudice Works Quietly

The dirty work of prejudice cannot always be
seen. With jokes, raised eyebrows, whisperings, gossip, humans playing god, and in a thousand subtle
ways this demonic idea keeps God's will from being
accomplished. Neighbors don't know each other.
Workmen sweat on each other and yet never move
beyond the niceties of politeness.

Prejudice keeps men strangers. Prejudice denies
brotherhood. Prejudice cannot even pronounce reconciliation.

The Bible simply says, "God is no respecter of
persons" (Acts 10:34, KJV). Prejudice shouts, "That
is a lie."

Idol Worship

Prejudice is a god worshiper. Its god is the external—skin, pigmentation, size of the nostrils, and
texture of the hair. These have become the altars
at which its life flows. Its values are found *only*
in what you can see with the eyes, touch with hands,
smell with the nose, and trace back through ancestry.
The sin of prejudice is that "it limits the personal
to the self alone." [3]

Prejudice endures a lonely death. It dies in a
wooden world no larger than its own backyard. Its
dimensions are bordered on the north, south, east,

3. *Ibid.*, p. 19.

and west by itself. Me, myself, and I are the only funeral attenders. The announcement in the local paper tells the tragedy. Please, no flowers, no neighbors, no friends, no loved ones, no Christ—this is a private affair.

The eulogy is pronounced by one, for prejudice is short. Why is the sun so red today? It is red with the blood of humanity. Prejudice never saw it, nor understood it, nor lived out these truths—"And He made from one [common origin, one source, one blood] *all* nations of men to settle on the face of the earth" (Acts 17:26, AMP).

Prejudice is a nobody because it did not share itself with anybody. It could never love its neighbor because it hated itself.

Only Beginnings

There is no ending to the definition of prejudice. There are only beginnings because prejudice is an idea looking for a mind in which to take root. This book and your presence within its pages indicates, "My heart is not available. Go to hell, prejudice, where you belong, with nonbeings, no God, no love, and no community. Go to hell, prejudice, where malice, envy, and perversion thrive. Go to hell, prejudice, where men are always falling—falling away from each, falling from themselves, making space between themselves and God. Alienation, separation, and brokenness are your handiwork. Stay there in the darkness of your aloneness. You can't live in the light of brotherhood."

3.
The Bible on Prejudice

Bob Shurden

The canonical literature of the so-called Judeo-Christian heritage does not include numerous, explicit references to the mind-set that we commonly refer to as *prejudice*. There is sufficient evidence, however, to warrant the conclusion that prejudicial treatment of persons is antithetical to the life of Christian righteousness regardless of the cause, if we never find it, and regardless of the cure, if we never find it. That antithesis is either implied, stated, or illustrated in several places in the Scriptures. It is implied in the Levitical and Deuteronomic legislation that Israelites in general and judges in particular "Do no injustice in judgment; . . . not be partial to the poor or defer to the great, but in righteousness shall you judge your neighbor" (Lev. 19:15, RSV). Or as Deuteronomy 1:17 states it: "You shall not be partial in judgment, you shall hear the small and the great alike; you shall not be afraid of the face of man, for the judgment is God's" (RSV).

Also, the prejudiced perspective is judged negatively when compared to the life-style of the incarnate one, Jesus the Christ.

Thirdly, the Scriptures illustrate what I see to be the agony of changing prejudicial feelings with the description of the pilgrimage of Simon Peter and his encounter with Cornelius.

And finally, the Christian disciple—the Christian brother is admonished and exhorted to nonprejudicial existence by James in a brief book that Martin Luther called "an epistle of straw."

In that book prejudice is decried with a parable of what I call the prejudiced congregation or the parable of the prejudiced assembly. I wanted first to call it the parable of the prejudiced usher until I discovered that James uses the plural "you" and not the singular. So he's speaking of a congregation as well as an usher.

The choice of the passage in James as the focus of our comments is determined by three factors. The term that the author of the book of James uses to describe the problem is a recurring one in the New Testament and is probably less ambiguous than our modern word prejudice.

He speaks of the problem or the sin of *prosopolempsia* which comes from two Greek words, *prosopon*, meaning face, and *lempsia* from *lambano*, meaning to receive. In other words, he speaks negatively about face-receiving.

Prosopolempsia is variously translated in the English versions as respect of persons, partiality, snobbery, or favoritism. But I like the Greek best— it's face-receiving. It's judging a person on the basis of appearance. So one reason I chose this passage as focal is because he used the word and it will recur in other places of the New Testament.

Secondly, the passage gives a very practical and concrete illustration of face-receiving. He talked about a congregation of Christian brothers where two men enter, one was rich, the other poor. And James said, "You pay attention to the rich man and you say to the poor man, 'Sit here on the floor by my feet.'" So he gives a very practical illustration of face-receiving. We don't have to look elsewhere. It's there.

And third, in this particular passage we have most of the basic arguments against prejudice in the Christian life. Many of these we'll find elsewhere, but this is truly a focal passage. It's one which seems to embody most of what we can say about the antithesis of the Christian life and prejudicial feelings.

It would probably be helpful for us now to read this focal passage. I am going to read from the *Revised Standard Version* where the word face-receiving is translated partiality. In the *Good News for Modern Man* it's translated, "You must never treat people in different ways because of their outward appearance" (Jas. 2:1, TEV). Now that's a whole lot of English trying to explain what one Greek word says—face-receiving or face acceptance.

So very important for our comments is the first thirteen verses of this focal passage of James.

My brethren, [and that's no insignificant beginning for people who are treating others unbrotherly] show no [face-receiving] partiality as you hold the faith of our Lord Jesus Christ, the Lord of glory. For if a man with gold rings and in fine clothing comes into your assembly, and a poor man in shabby clothes also comes in, and you pay attention to the one who wears the fine clothing and say, "Have a seat here, please," while you say to the poor man, "Stand there," or, "Sit at my feet," have you not made distinctions among yourselves, and become judges with evil thoughts? Listen, my beloved brethren. Has not God chosen those who are poor in the world to be rich in faith and heirs of the kingdom which he has promised to those who love him? But you have dishonored the poor man. Is it not the rich who oppress you, is it not they who drag you into court? Is it not they who blaspheme that honorable name by which you are called? If you really fulfil the royal law, according to the scripture, "You shall love your neighbor as yourself," you do well. But if you show partiality [if you receive faces], you commit sin, and are convicted by the law as transgressors. For whoever keeps the whole law but fails in one point has become guilty of all of it. For he who said, "Do not commit adultery," said also, "Do not kill." If you do not commit adultery but do kill, you have become a transgressor of the law. So speak and so act as those who are to be judged under the law of liberty. For judgment is without mercy to one who has shown no mercy; yet mercy triumphs over judgment (Jas. 2:1-13, RSV).

In this passage we note three basic premises, three basic arguments by which James demonstrated the antithesis of prejudice and the Christian life. Let me cite them briefly for you as subjects and then I will come back to them.

First of all, James talked about prejudice as it is related to the nature of God. Secondly, he spoke of prejudice as it is related to one's profession of faith. Third, he viewed prejudice from its relation to neighbor-love.

Prejudice and the nature of God. One of several of these bases for elimination of prejudice is theological in nature. Stated specifically, prejudice is a contradiction of the nature of God. On the matter of judging by appearance, the Scriptures are clear and emphatic with regard to deity. In 1 Samuel 16:7, Samuel is told, "Man looks on the outward appearance, but the Lord looks on the heart" (RSV). Peter's bout with prejudice found him concluding, "God has shown me that I should not call any man common or unclean" (Acts 10:28, RSV). "Truly I perceive that God shows no partiality, but in every nation anyone who fears him and does what is right is acceptable to him" (Acts 10:34-35, RSV). The apostle Paul, on more than one occasion, maintained that there is no face-receiving with God (Rom. 2:11; Eph. 6:9; Col. 3:25).

The Old Testament, Simon Peter, and the apostle Paul, all agree that the nature of God is impartiality. James asked the congregation a question. Note it in verse 5: "Listen, my beloved brethren. Has not

God chosen those who are poor in the world to be rich in faith and heirs of the kingdom which he has promised to those who love him? But you have dishonored the poor" (RSV).

Norman Snaith, in an intriguing little book, *The Distinctive Ideas of the Old Testament*, makes a comment that sometimes seems to be suggestive of prejudice. He said that in the Old Testament as well as the New Testament, God's righteous activity shows a bias in favor of the little folks. He maintained that the Scripture teaches that God is biased in favor of those who are the objects of prejudice. God takes the side of the powerless, the abused, the suspicioned, and the needy. That's his nature. His nature is to side with those who are getting kicked around. Yes, God's nature, even his name, is impartiality; because in the Old Testament as well as the New Testament, you know without my saying, one's name was indicative of his nature.

Consequently, let me suggest to you, as I think James was suggesting, that the greatest vulgarity amongst man is not using G-O-D and adding vulgar words, but it's living a life antithetical to the nature and name of God. We take God's name in vain by being the opposite of his moral qualities, one of which is impartiality. James said, "It's God's nature to choose the folks that you are rejecting."

There's something wrong when we as his children are to implement his nature and yet our life-style contradicts his name. James, however, was writing to Christians. He was not only writing to people who believed in God and who had a theology. He was writing to people who had a Christology. He was writing to a people who believed that in Christ, God had become present among them.

Hence, James discussed more than theology. In fact, he began his discussion with this statement: "My brethren show no [face-receiving] as you hold the faith of our Lord Jesus Christ," (Jas. 2:1, RSV). James implied by his opening admonition that the experience of faith in the lordship of Jesus is perverted by the practice of face-receiving.

It is characteristic of all New Testament writers that the truths they believed about God they saw enfleshed in the person of Jesus. Some commentators suggest to us that when James called Jesus "the Lord of glory," by "glory" James meant the splendor of God's presence as men are permitted to glimpse it.

Possibly sarcastically, but none the less factually, Jesus' opponents said to him on one occasion, "We know that you are truth." I believe that means, "We know that you are a man of integrity. And you care for no man, for you do not regard the position" (and the Greek word translated position there is *prosopon—face*). "For you do not regard the face of men." Even Jesus' opponents affirmed the fact that *he* was not a face-receiver.

Faith, then, in Jesus, one who was not a face-receiver, is more than believing *that* he is. Faith is a commitment to *what* he is. It is more than believing in his existence. It is a commitment and an openness and an obedience to *what* that existence is. It is commitment to *what* he is, *what* he says, *what* he stands for. What was he? Who was he? Well, he was one who made acceptance of others the condition for change rather than change of others the condition for acceptance. Jesus never said to others, "Change who and what you are and I'll accept you." He accepted them and said that's the basis for changing.

One of the several consistencies that I find in the life and ministry of Jesus is that he was constantly taking the side of the objects of other people's prejudices. It didn't matter whether they were shepherds or harlots, Samaritans or tax collectors, he was usually found pitching his tent with people other folks said were the wrong kind of people. That's where he liked to live. That's *what* he was. And faith in him is a commitment not only to the *fact* that he is but a commitment to *what* he is.

But another thing that I am reminded of—Jesus was one who was moved more by the needs of others than he was by his own ego needs. He was moved more by the needs of other selves than he was the needs of his own self. He was one who was more concerned about the survival and wholeness of persons than he was with the wholeness and survival of the institutions of Judaism, legalism, or race. Any time there was a choice to be made between institutions and people he consistently chose the latter. That's *what* he is. And faith in the lordship of Jesus over us is commitment to *what* he is as well as the belief *that* he is.

Finally, Jesus was and is one who believed sacrifice to be the way to the reversal of man's self-centeredness. It's interesting to me to note that both Jesus our Lord and Caiaphas, the high priest of the Sanhedrin which was the council that tried him, go on record as believing in the value of sacrifice. The high priest, Caiaphas, said on one occasion, "It is expedient [it is even necessary] for you that one man should die for the people" (John 11:50, RSV). Both Caiaphas and Jesus believed that. There was only one difference. Caiaphas believed in the sacrifice of others; Jesus believed in the sacrifice of self.

Prejudice and discrimination is the sacrifice of others. Openness and acceptance is the sacrifice of self. That's what he was. That's what he is. And faith in him is perverted when anything less than that is characteristic of us.

Prejudicial action, that is judgment on the basis of appearance to the point of dehumanization, is a contradiction of one's profession. James said it something like this, "Have you not made distinctions among yourselves?" (Jas. 2:4, RSV). And that's an interesting word which is translated "make distinctions." It's *diacreno*. It is a compound of two words, the prepositions, *dia* and *creno*, meaning to judge which is sometimes very accurately and very validly translated "make distinctions." But you know something else it can mean? *Diacreno* can mean "you have by your actions cut through yourself." *Dia* means "through." *Diacreno* can mean, "by your action you have judged through yourself." You've cut yourself in half. You've been inconsistent. You're wishy-washy. You've waivered. You've been two people. Prejudice is cutting through the profession of our faith in the Christ.

Finally, James maintained that prejudice is the antithesis of neighbor-love. In James 2:8-9, not accidentally it seems to me, after talking about prejudice, he begins to talk about neighbor-love. He contrasts the life of love for neighbor with prejudicial action.

One of these is the royal law, cited by Jesus as the essential ingredient in kingdom existence. Jesus said to the young man who wanted to know, "What's the summary of it all? What's the heart of it all? What's the core of it all?" Jesus said, "It's this: Love God with all of your heart, soul, mind and strength."

We could spend much time and space dividing man up and trying to find out what those are. But one thing I know he was saying, and that is, "Love God with everything that goes to make up self." But he also said, "The second is like unto the first, You love your neighbor as though he were you."

Love God with all of yourself. Love your neighbor as though he were yourself. That's it. James cited neighbor love as unrestricted concern and action in the interest of other people. Paul as well as James saw the normativeness of *agape*. As I've studied in the New Testament, I find it to be best defined as "willing the well-being of others regardless of their merit and your cost."

James is so direct as to say, "If you show partiality, if you receive faces, you commit sin." Face-receiving is sin because it is the opposite of love. Face-receiving is sin because it's self-love. Face-receiving is the opposite and antithesis of *agape* because *agape* is being other centered and face-receiving is self-exalting.

James didn't tell us what causes prejudice. He didn't tell us the cure; I wish he had. But I do know with as much clarity as anyone can present it that he said, "It's the antithesis of God; it's the antithesis of Christian profession of faith; it's the antithesis of neighbor love." How can we keep prejudice and sacrifice all three of those?

4.
Does the Difference Make a Difference?

Dick Brogan

(*Acts 10:28; Rom. 10:12*).

I can identify with Simon Peter. He and I have a great deal in common—quick tongue, quick temper, slow to learn (Ph.D. in ignorance), and doing graduate work in ignorance. I, too, am quick to opinionate. I saw this prayer recently: "Forgive me this day my daily opinion. Forgive me the one I had yesterday."

Peter Believed in Difference

Simon Peter first believed *the difference does make a difference!* Peter was a Jew. He faithfully followed Jewish traditions and laws. Every Jew believed that God had no use for Gentiles. Ancient Jews thought God favored the Jews and the Jews alone. There was such an emotional dislike for Gentiles that a Jew would not help a Gentile woman in time of childbirth because that activity would only bring another Gentile into the world. Gentiles were the fuel for the fires of hell—so thought the ancient Jews. Every Jew prayed this morning prayer:

"I thank Thee, O Lord, that I am not a slave, not a woman, not a Gentile."

God Deals with Peter's Prejudice

Peter's staying with Simon, who was a tanner, was God's initial dealing with Peter's prejudice. God was dealing with his Jewishness! A tanner had to touch dead animals. The touching of any dead object would make Simon unclean. A Jew would only eat animals that chewed a cud and whose hooves were cloven (split).

Peter went to the rooftop and while there experienced a vision—the sheet let down by four corners was full of four-footed animals, reptiles, and birds. These were the kind his dietary rules would not allow him to enjoy at the dining table.

"Get up, Peter, and kill and eat."

"No, Lord, I have never eaten anything impure or unclean. I keep the laws of my fathers, traditions of my culture, customs of my ancestors."

"Don't call anything impure God has made! All that I have made has *purpose, design,* and *dignity.* Haven't you learned that everything I have made is distinct? It's an original, authentic. No two snowflakes are alike, no two animals. But difference doesn't mean better than or more important than. All of my creation points to purpose and beauty. The difference doesn't make a difference, Simon."

Life Is Unlearning

I am like Peter in several ways. (1) *I continually*

have to unlearn some things my culture taught me.
Most of life has to be spent *unlearning*. Some culture
is good—but most of it needs close examination. A
person can be wrongly taught. You don't have to
teach a child to be bad; you teach him to do good.

The Tanners and Corneliuses Are Sent to Us

God sends many tanners and Corneliuses to teach
us truths. Some of the messengers are old, some
young, and some black. Life is an educational ven-
ture, pilgrimage. The classroom is the world—*who
taught me what I now believe?* Does not learning
mean changing?

Three Visions to Change Peter

(1) *It takes me several visions before I will believe.*
The Lord used three visions, and repeated experi-
ences to help Peter see the light. Show me again.
Tell me again. The human is stubborn. It takes a
lot of visions and encounters for most of us. God
persists that we accept all his creatures as kinfolk.

(2) *All are clean.* God made them. Do we only
accept persons who live up to our culture or standards? But all persons are acceptable. This is the
point of the vision. We have trouble separating a
man from his sins. God sees a man apart from his
wrongs. He measures potential. We label a man as
a sinner, a drunkard, a gambler, etc. She is a gossip
or a prostitute. Jesus talked in terms of personal
wholeness. He taught a relational gospel. Forgive
your enemies. Love your neighbors. Go the second

mile. Turn the other cheek. Don't judge. All these require an "other" orientation and life-style.

(3) *All of us are unique.* God only made one of you—no carbons. You can look, feel, act, or live as a liberated human being, but your difference shouldn't make a difference in relationships with others. Through grace and mercy we can accept and respect another person's differences.

These words penned by an unknown poet ask the ultimate question: What's a human being worth?

What's a Man Worth?

What's a man worth?
Does anyone know?
Is he measured by riches,
By friend or foe?
Can we tell by his virtues,
His station in life?
His accent? His color?
His peace, or his strife?
The length of his hair,
The shape of his nose,
His smile or his handshake
The cut of his clothes?
What's a man worth?
We turn to our Guide.
And Christ gives His answer
"For each man I died."

5.
Finding Self in the Divine Encounter

S. L. Bowman

(*Luke 8:26-39*).

The Black Church and Human Justice

I want to share with you a passage of Scripture which seems to be analogous to the history of the black man in America. In concentrating on these verses, we need to keep in mind that the black church has been in the forefront of the struggle for human decency and justice from its very beginning. The black church takes the position that the purpose or reason for which the church exists is not salvation alone, but liberation as well.

The story of slavery in this country has always been fascinating to me. Some pseudointellectuals, both black and white, have sought to remove this disgraceful chapter from our history by denying that it ever happened, but slavery is a fact in American history. Out of this disgraceful chapter of our history a movement was begun that has grown into an institution—the black church. The black church, like every other movement in history, has stirred concern and got the attention of the people in the community because it is authentic and original.

Spectators or Participators

There are several key verses in this passage that I would like to briefly analyze. Verse 35 says, "Then they went out to see what was done." They didn't go out to learn, just to see. They didn't go out to show their appreciation to Jesus for what he had done, but to see. They didn't go out to participate in the day's activities or to become involved in the healing process of their neighbor and friend, but just to see. Here is where we draw the line between the role we play in life and history.

Some people become and remain eternal spectators. They just go out to see. You can see them standing on the sidelines of every demonstration and great movement in history. They just want to see. I sometimes wonder what answer will be given when their children and grandchildren ask, "Where were you when this movement was taking place?" "Then they went out to see what was done." Some even come to church that way. They come just to see. They can tell you whose voice was pitched in the wrong key. They can tell you whose shoes and bag didn't match. They can tell you whose subject and verb didn't agree. They just see.

The question is or should be: Where will I stand in history? Will I stand as a spectator or as a participator? "Then they went out to see what was done."

Fear of Wholeness

Luke said three things about the man in the text. He was (1) at the feet of Jesus. This is indicative of the fact that he knew something of the value of worship. Luke said he was "sitting at the feet of Jesus" (v. 35). (2) Clothed. This is just the opposite of being naked. He was not naked physically or symbolically. (3) In his right mind. He was, as the youth of today would say—together. He had been made whole because he had had this divine encounter.

The latter part of verse 35 gives us some insight into the character of the people who lived in Gadara, Luke said "and they were afraid." Don't you think it's interesting that his particular statement comes after we had been informed about this man's humiliating experience? Luke said that "he was sitting at the feet of Jesus, clothed, and in his right mind: and they were afraid." This is indicative of the fact that while the man was being destroyed by a legion of demons, while he was naked and not ashamed, while he didn't know Jesus, himself, or anyone else, no one seems to have been concerned about him. His neighbors ignored him and pretended that he didn't exist. He was not a member of the intelligentsia and his name was not in the social register, therefore he was not important, or so it seemed to his neighbors. But when they found him with his clothes on, when they found him sitting at the feet of Jesus, when they found him together, they were afraid.

Those of us who are students of history can draw an analogy here. As long as we were picking cotton in Mississippi and Alabama, working in the sugar-cane fields of Lousiana, picking watermelons in Smith County of Mississippi, cooking, ironing, washing, and baby-sitting for white families all over this country, laughing when we were not tickled (no, we were not laughing, we were grinning), America was satisfied. If I were giving a lecture in black studies, I would tell you the difference between a laugh and a grin. A laugh comes from the inside and expresses joyous fulfillment, but a grin is external and is an escape mechanism. As long as we were saying "yes sir" and "yes ma'am," when we really wanted to say "———— No!," America was satisfied. But one day America looked up and saw us standing before the Supreme Court interpreting the law much better than those who wrote it, and without the contradictions that George Washington and Thomas Jefferson had in their lives.

A Fear Response

After the Revolutionary War, George Washington, rather than trying to build up a free nation, was in New York looking for runaway slaves. When Patrick Henry uttered the immortal words, "Give me liberty or give me death," he too had slaves. I have often wondered what Patrick Henry would have done when he said, "Give me liberty or give me death," if one of his slaves had come into that assembly and said, "Me, too."

One day America saw us marching to the ballot boxes, sitting down at lunch counters, riding at the front of busses and sleeping in hotels and motels, and all America became afraid. As this movement started by the church continued, every community in this nation found it necessary to spend more money for police equipment. They started training men all over the nation in how to shoot better, not to think better. "And they found the man out of whom the devils were departed, sitting at the feet of Jesus, clothed, and in his right mind: they were afraid."

The Black Identity Crisis

The man in the text was lost. Somewhere in his life tragedy had befallen him. In his concept of humanism, Elton Trueblood would say he became a sort of "cut flower." He could not handle the ordinary, everyday problems he faced. "What is your name?" Jesus asked. He came up with a weird answer, "My name is Legion, for we are many." Howard Thurman suggested that while this man was responding to Jesus, a thought ran through his mind, "That's my trouble. I don't know my name. I don't know who I am. There are so many of me that I don't know which me the real me is. My name is Legion! I'm lost. I don't know who I am." When you are inwardly lost, the logical question is, "Who am I?" When you are outwardly lost, the logical question is, "Where am I?" This man didn't know who he was, and he didn't know where he was. He was what J. Robert Bradley calls "A Poor Pilgrim of Sorrow."

I'm a poor pilgrim of sorrow lost in this world all alone, no hope have I for tomorrow, I'm trying to make heaven my home.

Sometime I feel so discouraged, sometime I don't know where I can roam, But I heard of a city they call heaven, I've started to make heaven my home.

My mother has reached that bright glory, my father is still walking in sin, my brothers and sisters won't own me, because I've been born again.

This is the black man's situation in America. I would like to ask the black man in America, "What is your name?" His response is poetic but factual: "They brought me from the land of my birth, didn't ask me my name, but gave me one. I don't know who I am. Some people call me nigger, but that's not my name. Some call me boy, and I have already lived two score years. Some even call me uncle, but they are not my nieces and nephews. I don't know who I am." At this point the apostle Paul comes to his rescue and says, "Therefore if any man be in Christ, he is a new creature: old things are passed away; behold all things are become new" (2 Cor. 5:17).

I remember an incident that happened early in my childhood. One day two men at church almost came to blows because one called the other out of his name. One of the deacons of my membership church tried to shame the men for having acted in such a fashion. "But he called me out of my name," was the response from the offended brother. At that point, the deacon made a statement that is redemptive in the finest sense of the word: "You don't have to be what he called you."

A Sickness in Society

Not only was the man in the text lost, but he was a sick man. He was sick unto death. He was in a state between life and death. He was too dead to be alive and too alive to be dead. He was afflicted with a despondency that is indeed sickness unto death. Look at what he had lost. He had lost his identity, purpose, hope, integrity, and dignity. When one has lost these he is sick unto death. Now the other side of the coin is responsibility. Who was responsible for this man's condition? When any man helps to destroy another man's purpose, slaughter another man's dreams, that man is more than sick unto death. He is a murderer, guilty of genocide. When a man is sick he needs more than an antibiotic. He needs healing.

We can't very well concentrate on the sickness of the man without considering the sickness of the world around him. Yes, he was sick, but so was the world. One has only to read the record of the man as given by Luke to be thoroughly convinced that the world around him was sick also. He was an insane

man living in an insane world. His community didn't
provide him with housing, therefore he had his
dwelling in the graveyard. They provided no institution to deal with his mental health. He needed love,
care, attention, and they gave him chains. They
attempted to lock him up, but instead they locked
him out—out of the community's social, civic, and
religious life. Then they criticized him for mis-
behaving. He was an insane man in an insane world.

I submit to you that we are still living in an insane
world. This must be a crazy world. A world that
will send a boy to a detention center charged with
juvenile delinquency for stealing a loaf of bread
because he's hungry and then pardon a President
for abusing the powers of the highest political office
in the world must be crazy. A world that would
assassinate a John F. Kennedy and then run a George
Wallace for President must be a crazy world!

Finding Sanity

The man in the text was an insane or crazy man
passing through the "valley" of which all blacks are
too well acquainted. As a boy I heard my grand-
mother sing about this valley. She said, "You've got
to walk that lonesome valley, you've got to walk
it for yourself, there is nobody here can walk it for
you; you've got to walk it for yourself." No one is
exempt from walking this valley.

Dr. Harry Emerson Fosdick, professor of preaching at Union Theological Seminary in New York
City, 1915-1946, and eminent pastor of Riverside

Church in New York, tells in his autobiography, *The Living of These Days,* how he had to walk the valley. He was fresh out of college and engaged to be married. For some reason he became despondent and entertained the thought of suicide. One night as he attempted to follow through with his plan of suicide with a razor at his throat, his father called him, "Harry, Harry!" There was something in Mr. Fosdick's voice that apparently changed young Harry's mind. When you are sick, insane, if someone close by you can keep on calling you by your right name, you can find the way through the valley.

What happened to the man? He met the young teacher from Nazareth. Nazareth, because of its strategic position as a crossroad, had gotten a bad reputation. It was a high crime area because of its traffic in prostitution and the low economic status of its citizenry. Because of these factors and others, it was said that nothing good could come out of Nazareth. Yet this man who needed help so desperately found God, found himself, and found the healing he needed when he met the Christ of Nazareth. Jesus looked at him with love, reached out to him with brotherhood, and pulled him in with purpose. Love, brotherhood, and purpose embraced him and for the first time he felt like somebody.

A Rallying Center for Human Rights

Howard Thurman describes this spirit of some-bodyness for the black man in his book *The Luminous Darkness.* Dr. Thurman's book deals with the black church and how it provides integrity and a sense of somebodyness to black people. He said, "It is a great irony that the Negro church has figured so largely as a rallying center for the civil rights movement in the South primarily because its religious experience in the Negro church made it inevitable. For a long time the Negro church was the one place in the life of a people which was comparatively free from interference by the white community. A man may be buffeted about by his environment or may be regarded as a nobody in the general community. A woman may be a nurse in a white family in which their three-year-old child in her care calls her by her first name, thus showing quite unconsciously that this is the context in which she is held by his parents. This Negro man and woman come to their church and for one fulfilling moment they are somebody."

When the man met Jesus he wanted to stay with Jesus. Perhaps because Jesus was the only one to give recognition to his somebodyness. In addition to his somebodyness being recognized by Jesus, something had happened to this man. If we were to ask William Jones he would probably say he had reorientation of his personality. E. Stanley Jones would say he had his "master motive" changed. Paul Tillich would say he was grasped by an ultimate concern. The New Testament would simply say he was "born again."

The Divine Encounter

I am not sufficiently sophisticated at this point

to really describe for you and to you what happened to this man. Permit me to borrow the black conversion experience of bygone years to help you gain some insight into what happened to the man in the text. Our ancestors would simply say, "I was in sorrow's valley, with my head hung down like a bulrush in the morning. I was on a downward road, no hat on my head, no shoes on my feet, no God on my side, and no heaven in my view. I was too mean to live and not fit to die. The handcuffs of hell were on my hands, the shackles of damnation on my feet, but I saw Jesus hanging on Calvary's cross, dying for a sin sick world. He spoke peace to my dying soul, turned me around, cut loose my stammering tongue and sent me on my way. Ever since that day, I have been rising and falling, but I made my vow to the Lord and I will never turn back no more. I'm going to run on and see what the end is going to be."

P. E. Lott, veteran preacher in the state of Mississippi, describes the conversion experience thusly: "I was sin sick. I went to Dr. Conscience. He wrote me out a prescription of hospital redemption. He put me on the operating table, took the knife of the Holy Spirit and operated on my heart. He washed my soul in the laver of regeneration. He soaked it in faith and rinsed it in grace. He put it on the rub board of prayer, rubbed it, rubbed it and kept on rubbing it. He hung it on the line of love and dried it with the sunlight of His own dear Son. He sprinkled it with the dewdrops of the Holy Spirit. He took it down and put it on the ironing board of truth. He took it down and ironed out all the wrinkles. When he got through, he folded it real nice and put it into the wardrobe of God's eternal providence, and ever since that day I have been telling the world He's mine."

"Then they went out to see what was done; and came to Jesus, and found the man, out of whom the devils were departed, sitting at the feet of Jesus, clothed and in his right mind: and they were afraid." The casting out of the legion of devils caused quite a stir in Gadara. The keepers of the swine had reported the incident as well as the loss of the herd. The Gadarenes came, looked on and asked Jesus to leave their country. Before departing, Jesus made a request of the man who had been made whole. " 'Go home and tell how much God has done for you.' So the man left and preached all over the town how much Jesus had done for him" (Luke 8:39, Beck).

Telling the Story

Yes, Jesus gave the Gadarene demoniac a story to tell—a story of what God has done for us in Jesus Christ his Son. Each person who finds himself through divine encounter is given this story to tell. It is an old story, but it is a true story. It is the story of one who was rich, but for our sakes he became poor, that we through his poverty might be rich. He was born in another man's stable, grew up in another man's home, worked in another man's carpenter shop, and preached from another man's boat. He rode another man's donkey into town, instituted the Lord's Supper in another man's upper room, died for other men's sins, was buried in another man's grave—a borrowed grave of a friend, and on the morning of the third day he rose for other men's justification. He took the sting from death, the victory from the grave, and declared, "All power is in my hands." I don't know about you, but I, too, like the man of Gadara have a story to tell. I love to tell the story. Do you?

My Story

The story I have to tell is what God in Jesus Christ has done for me, and if given a chance will do for you. I grew up in rural Mississippi in what has been called a racist society. In this society the white man had his place and the black man had his place. Neither was expected to invade the private domain of the other. Rather, they were both expected to acquiesce to community standards and stay in their separate places. Whites who acted too friendly toward blacks were branded as nigger lovers, and blacks were considered Uncle Toms, and became suspect by other blacks, who labeled them as white mouthed and, therefore, were not to be trusted. I grew up against this kind of background.

Whites Are Not the Only Prejudiced People

I suppose the biggest mistake I have ever made in life or will make was to believe for a long time that only whites were prejudiced. As long as I felt this way I failed to recognize that not only were there racists and extremists among blacks, but that I, myself, had some racial hangups. We are taught in counseling that one must first recognize that he has a problem; second, identify the problem; and, third, find a solution to the problem. As much as I hated to admit it, even to myself, I had to confess that Samuel Bowman had some prejudices.

The Answer to Prejudice

I need not belabor the point that the answer to racial prejudice is the love of God as revealed in Jesus Christ his Son. I came to recognize, what I had always somehow believed, that the gospel is for all men regardless of their racial identity.

Through my involvement with the Department of Cooperative Ministries with National Baptists of the Mississippi Baptist Convention Board, the Mississippi Baptist Seminary, the Billy Graham Mississippi Crusade, and, last but not least, the Greater Clark Street Baptist Church, I have tried to implement the principles of the gospel of Jesus Christ in my own life. This gospel is the gospel of love. Because of this, I can say with great meaning:

I like to see a man who is black, conscious of his color and appreciates the fact.

I like to see a man who is white. Everybody has a color, any color is alright.

I like to see a person who understands that character makes the person, color does not make a man.

6.
My Confession of Errors

Dick Brogan

I am confessing my errors in relationships with black people. For almost fifteen years I have worked for the Home Mission Board and the Mississippi Baptist Convention Board in its mission program among National Baptists (the denominational name for black Baptists). I wish I could say that I have done everything right . . . but you are too smart to swallow that tale. Here are some errors I've made in race relations. The list is incomplete but I have tried to be fair and honest with myself and you. Will you hear a Mississippian and my errors in race relations?

Error No. 1 *I believed culture and tradition were divine.* We all grow up believing in grown-ups. But tradition and culture are man-made. Much of what we believe about our fellowman is based on myth, source, distance, prejudice, and not fact. I have been amazed at how many of the things I was taught about blacks were untrue. Most of these mistaken ideas have been blown out of the mythical water by the last fifteen years of personal relationships. Ideas I had about blacks' intelligence, cleanliness, and laziness have been refuted by the facts.

Man is responsible for tradition and culture—not God. I had to believe either what culture taught or what the Scripture said. I was like Simon Peter in his experience with Cornelius. I had to look at my prejudices. Listen to Peter's words: "You yourselves know very well that a Jew is not allowed by his religion to visit or associate with a Gentile. But God has shown me that I must not consider any man unclean or defiled" (Acts 10:28, TEV).

Error No. 2 *I thought that I had to always be the giver in a racial relationship.* Most of the mission efforts of whites around the world are based upon the idea that we are givers and that other races are the receivers. This is a relationship usually based upon paternalism—a parent-child relationship. I do the talking—minorities do the listening. I must be the giver—minorities do the receiving.

I remember one time after I had spoken in a black church they took up a small offering. I didn't want to take it until an old man said, "Don't you think our money is good enough for you?" It suddenly dawned on me that I must receive if a growing relationship was to continue.

The black church has made many contributions to my life. Namely, the freedom to worship, using body, voice, and mind, helped to set me free from too much ritual, formality, and coldness. I am thankful for the opportunity to have been a taker from the richness of the black church heritage. Some of the most creative, imaginative preaching I have experienced has come to me by way of the black church.

I am in debt. My life has been blessed, filled full by exposure to the Negro church. I have laughed, cried, felt joy, and have experienced affirmation in the presence of my black brothers and sisters.

Error No. 3 *I was naive in assuming that only white people have racial prejudices.* I know that might be a revelation of my ignorance, but for many years I thought prejudice was only a white man's problem.

One Sunday I made my way to a speaking engagement at a black church in the Mississippi Delta. After finding the church I was escorted to the platform. After being seated and speaking to the pastor, who was a friend of many years, I heard the voice of a 4-year-old girl who posed this question to her mother, "What is that white man doing here?" For the first time in my life I realized that prejudice can enter anybody's mind. Blacks feel and exhibit prejudice. I have felt the cold eyes of rejection. I know the meaning of discrimination, too. I have walked the path of racism as a giver and a taker. I have known oppression by the oppressed.

Error No. 4 *I thought that God's world of people was only an enlarged version of my own backyard.* But I learned God is so much larger than I can conceive him to be. He is God of infinite variety. I was so local, so provincial, so slow to see that he came to save a whole world of humanity. I know he came for me, but how slow I was to admit he came to give himself to every man.

Simon Peter's words again: "I now realize that it is true that God treats all men alike. Whoever fears him and does what is right is acceptable to him, no matter what race he belongs to" (Acts 10:34, TEV).

Every person is not like me! Each man is different—color, background, politics, economics, family, religion, culture, genetics—but God, through Jesus Christ, came to affirm and forgive every man. ALL . . . He came to all, for all—he is incarnated because of all. This little selfish clod of human flesh and spirit had to learn that. I continually must remind myself that he loves each person in this entire universe as much as he loves me.

Error No. 5 *I believed that I could change my attitudes in my own strength.* Right racial attitudes come from what Carlyle Marney refers to as "private church." By "private church" I mean those heroes of my faith both dead and alive that help me to put aside cultural upbringing. By "private church" I mean teachers, urgings of the Holy Spirit, Scriptures, friends, and family that help a person to say no to fences of culture, religion, and power, when so often those structures are blind to God's truth.

How did I change—not only because of laws, supreme courts, marches, demonstrations, or sit-ins; but because of a continual audience (continual dialogue) with my "private church." I had to realize that the race problem is a spiritual blindness. Only God can cut away the cataracts to let me see his creation. I continually have to fight prejudice. In my life racism has to be uprooted and destroyed. It is like taking the garbage out every day at home. None of us would think of putting that rotting debris into our closets or in the corner of the room. We need to dispose of prejudice as it gathers. I am fighting not to let it use me.

It was an ancient rabbi who asked his students how they could tell when night had ended and the day was on its way back.

"Could it be when you see an animal in the distance and can tell whether it is a sheep or a dog?"

"No," answered the rabbi.

"Could it be when you look at a tree in the distance and can tell whether it is a fig tree or a peach tree?"

"No," answered the rabbi.

"Well, then, when is it?" the students demanded.

"It is when you look on the face of any woman or man and see that she or he is your brother or sister. Because if you cannot do this then no matter what time it is, it is still night." [1]

1. Joseph T. Nolan, ed. *Good Newsletter* Vol. IV, Issue 4, April 1977, Communications Center, p. 145.

7.
My Pilgrimage

Owen Cooper

(*By permission from the Home Mission Board*).

This is not an easy subject for me to discuss. It points up a spiritual deficit in my own life, and confessions do not come easy with me. It is on a subject that is not universally popular. Some take offense at any discussion about race. I believe this continues to be one of several problems sapping the strength and the spiritual vitality of Southern Baptists.

I am going to relate something of my pilgrimage in the area of race relations and make a few practical suggestions that I hope will be of particular interest to Southern Baptist lay people.

The problem of race relations still exists with many individual members of Southern Baptist churches, with many Southern Baptist churches, and with many organizations representing Southern Baptist churches.

I want to say that I believe the next major thrust in the area of improving interracial attitudes, action, and cooperation among Southern Baptists awaits the involvement of lay people. Many pastors have pioneered in this area. Now it is time for lay persons to become involved in the consideration of improved race relations.

I was raised on a hill farm about ten miles northeast of Vicksburg, Mississippi. We had a relatively large tract of land, but did not have what might be considered as a successful farming operation. There were a number of workmen and tenants on the farm, some white families and some black families. I grew up amidst all the tradition of segregation, discrimination, and denial of civil rights that was prevalent during my boyhood. This all became a part of my attitude and my culture. I don't know why I was not spiritually sensitive to the wrong that was in the system, but I was not.

It was years later, even after the 1954 decision of the Supreme Court, that my conscience began to stir. I began to ask questions about the right and wrong of the system under which we were operating. The reasoning I had built up to maintain my position began to melt away in the light of an open-minded search of the Scripture and the Christian conviction that all people are equal in the sight of God.

My children were a great deal of help to me, for they were far ahead of me in the application of Christian principles in the area of race. The action of the Southern Baptist Convention, which was ahead of me at that time, also gave me pause to think.

With time my thinking changed, my attitude changed, and my actions changed. This was a gradual process over a period of years; and it is still taking place.

I would like to make some suggestions or conclusions growing out of my experience in race relations. These are not suggested as any panacea, but they have been of interest and help to me.

(1) There came a time when I needed to reexamine my attitudes in the light of the Scripture. This I did. Now I know you can get "proof-text" from the Scripture to substantiate almost any position you take on most subjects. This is what I had been doing, but a time came when I tried to look at the teachings and works of Jesus in their entirety. When I considered the cumulative impact of his teachings and ministry in the light of my then-existing attitude toward race, I came to the conclusion that I was wrong.

When the total impact of Christ's teachings and ministry came in confrontation with the provincial and restricted attitude I had toward race, particularly members of the black race, my ideas lost the battle.

(2) I appeared before the Resolutions Committee of the Southern Baptist Convention many years ago, asking them to act negatively on a very mild resolution in the area of race relations. I served on several pulpit committees in our church and have polled prospective pastors in the area of race relations for fear that they might say something that would rock the boat.

Now I am ready for the Convention to speak boldly in the area of race relations and have supported recent actions in doing so. I am ready now for my pastor to speak out from the pulpit, as the Spirit may direct, in this still sensitive area.

Incidentally, it has always been interesting to me how careful a Southern Baptist church is to be sure that God "calls" a minister to the pulpit. Yet often, we would restrict the minister's freedom in the pulpit. I believe that a God-called man has a God-given message. Is it possible that God will call the minister without calling the message also? I want a God-called minister with a God-called message. I am willing to give him freedom in the pulpit on this or any other subject, although I may not fully agree with what he says.

(3) I am no longer afraid to talk about the subject of race. I talk about it at home; I talk about it at church; I talk about it with business groups. The subject is no longer taboo.

For too long, probably because of the fear of being misunderstood, or criticized, Southern Baptists ignored the problem of race. We need to come to understand the problem, not ignore it. A problem of this nature won't disappear because it is ignored.

(4) There came a time in my pilgrimage when I began to ask myself "Am I contributing to the race problem or am I becoming a part of the solution?" It appeared that for me my former attitudes and actions were not right. What should I do about it?

At first I took a negative attitude. I did not want to hurt the situation, but I did not want to become involved in a solution. I simply did nothing. I did a considerable amount of praying, little talking, and took no action. There swirled around me in the Southern Baptist Convention various opinions, many of them conflicting. I was standing on the sidelines. This is contrary to my nature, and before long I decided to get involved.

I began to ask myself "What can I do as a Southern Baptist layman in connection with this problem?" Here are some things I believe Southern Baptist lay people can do:

1. Unmuzzle your pastor. Let him know that insofar as you are concerned, he has freedom to speak his heart on the race question or any other matter. Let him know you believe that when God called him as a minister, he also called his message.

2. Get your church, or some segment of the church, to engage in some activity on Race Relations Sunday. This may be a small meeting of people in your home for prayer. It might be a discussion at a Church Training session. Or it might be encouraging the pastor to bring a message in one of the worship services on Race Relations.

3. Read some Christian material on the subject of race and prayerfully study the Scriptures to find Jesus' words and attitudes about race. Ask the Holy Spirit to guide your attitude and action in race relations.

4. Try to have a better understanding of the attitude of blacks toward whites. It is always well to understand the other fellow's position. You may not agree with him, but you can better meet the prob-

lems in relationships if you understand his attitude, his hang-ups, his frustrations, his dreams, and his ideas. One way to do this is by reading some books written by blacks, from the viewpoint of blacks.

5. Get to know several blacks who are your peers, intellectually and spiritually. Most of us simply do not know an educated, spiritually mature black person who has ideas and articulates them, who loves God and can discuss his religion intelligently. Getting to know persons of this nature would do more to break our stereotyped concept of black people than any other one thing. You should take the initiative in establishing such a contact, providing periodic opportunities for the friendship to develop.

6. Get involved in some religious project that involves both white and black people—perhaps a joint laymen's meeting for information, inspiration, and fellowship. Perhaps a prayer service, evangelistic meeting, crusade, tract distribution program, *agape* meal, nightwatch service or some type of enlargement campaign would promote cooperation.

7. Get personally involved in assisting one black toward greater achievements, particularly at a spiritual level. This could be to assist a student to go to school (particularly to study for the ministry), to participate in semester student missionary work, or to attend a conference such as the Baptist World Alliance Youth Congress; helping a struggling black church in a building program; buying books for a pastor's library; or helping a lay person attend a state or national convention.

8. Consider getting involved in some government

program directed toward helping poverty or low income groups. This could be in the area of housing, health, education, preschool child care, tutoring, literacy program, etc. This offers a perfect laboratory for learning, for understanding, and for help. If there is no such program in your area, you might lead in initiating one.

9. If you are a business person or have a business-related skill, consider involvement with a black enterprise. The challenge of the free enterprise system is as real to blacks as it is to whites. The ratio of people with management skills is much less among blacks than it is among whites. This causes a problem, but it creates a unique opportunity for whites to help blacks develop needed management skills and techniques.

Pride of ownership and the satisfaction of participating is greatly increasing among blacks, but they want to own businesses, in whole or in part, and to participate in management. You can help provide these opportunities.

10. Many black Baptist churches would welcome leadership in conducting a lay training school (WIN), a stewardship campaign, a study on how to establish and operate a church budget, the role of a deacon, the role of a lay person, etc.

This is not an all-inclusive list but simply some suggestions to indicate areas where a committed Southern Baptist lay person can become involved in a manner that will add to his knowledge, improve his understanding and contribute to the spiritual and physical well-being of blacks. The learning process is a two-way street, for blacks also have something to offer and something to teach.

I would not impose my thinking or suggestions on any lay person. That method generally stirs up animosity and resistance. A Southern Baptist's position on race is on a volunteer basis, but that does not mean it is unimportant.

Southern Baptists have made many proclamations and resolutions about race relations. Most Southern Baptist pastors are ready to move in the area, even beyond the limits they think exist in the minds of the deacons or the congregation. The missing ingredient is commitment and involvement on the part of Southern Baptist lay people. The lay person is the key to the situation.

8.
Your Lazarus Is at the Window

Dick Brogan

(*Luke 16:19-31*).

This passage is a story of contrasts. It is a story of the rich and the poor, the fed and the hungry, the haves and the have-nots, heaven and hell. It has some very serious implications for you and me as Christian workers in the twentieth-century church.

The Man Who Owned the Gate

"Dives" means rich. He was rich in a material sense. He had houses. He had threads. He had bread. But according to Jesus he was very poor—poor in relationships, in righteousness—poor in spirit—in attitudes.

We need to ask ourselves as church persons—when is a man rich? When is a man successful? These are questions people still ask today. A man is rich when he has appropriated the love of God known in Jesus Christ. We can share with them whatever we have experienced of his grace and mercy to make them rich in spirit.

A Man of Distinction

For his day he was well-dressed. He wore the very expensive. We must again ask ourselves, "Do clothes make a man?" When God judges a man he looks on the inside—not what he has, but what he is!

In this very materialistic day in which we live, a poet asked:

There are a number of us who creep into the world to eat and sleep, and know no reason why we are born, save only to consume the corn, devour the cattle, flock, sheep and fish, and leave behind an empty dish.

This man was well-clothed on the outside, but he was not clothed with the righteousness of God on the inside. If a man does not have character, goodness, and virtue, then Jesus Christ has not entered his life. A man is naked spiritually until Jesus Christ clothes him with his robe of goodness.

How does he treat others? How does he treat his neighbor? This is what distinguishes him in the spiritual world—not what he has on the outside, but the kind of man he is on the inside.

A Gate Is to Keep out and to Keep in

He was also a man with a gate. Now a gate says

that there is a fence and a fence indicates two main purposes—to keep out and to keep in.

I sometimes think that the twentieth-century church is much like this rich man. We have kept ourselves in. We have kept our witness in. We have kept our preaching in. We have kept our church activities in. One reason, perhaps, we have not exploded the Christian gospel in the world is because it has been as inside gospel.

Jesus—an Outside Man

Jesus was an outside man. He preached, taught, and ministered outside the institutional center. He related to outside people—Gentiles, Samaritans, tax collectors.

Are you keeping somebody out of your life? Is your life filled with separating fences and doors? I think we must all ask ourselves the question, "Is my church locked in or is it sending the gospel out? Get out of the huddle! The church has been gathered too long!

Filled but Hungry

He was a man who ate the best food. Some live to eat and some eat to live. But I wonder sometimes if those around us are not spiritually hungry. Although they may not look fat on the outside, they may have too much food to eat on their dining room tables. I wonder if they are not starving for the "bread of life" who is Jesus Christ. This man was interested only in himself.

Barclay recalled that "Edith lived in a world bound on the north, the south, the east and the west by Edith" because she was the center of her world.

Sometimes the church of Jesus Christ must reorientate itself. What are the priorities of your church? What are the priorities of your ministry? What are you really in the business of doing? What is your objective? What is your goal?

The Man Outside the Fence

Look at the man who was laid by the gate. His name was Lazarus. It is interesting that the word Lazarus means "God is my help." Sometimes God is the only one who does care about a person in this world. Jesus was always caring for those about him. He was moved with compassion toward people. He was moved by the world's pain. How many times did lepers and blind men stop him? He was moved by the world's loneliness—the woman at the well. He was moved by the world's condition and man-made religion. The scribes and Pharisees were using God to cover up their unrighteousness.

Do you and I have that kind of compassion? Do we care? Are we concerned about persons? The man who was laid by the gate was a beggar; he had nothing; he was helpless.

I am thinking that near your church there are those who are starving for love and care. I wonder if we are going to be the kind of Christians who will share the warmth, the compassion, and the love of Jesus Christ with those near us.

Dogs Licked Sores

The Bible said he could not even push the street dogs away from his sores. The Bible tells us in this story that the dogs came and licked his wounds. The dogs were more interested in his welfare than the human beings in the story.

There are so many who are diseased with meaninglessness and purposelessness, who are dying daily with a disease called sin, selfishness, and separation from God. Call it the breath of God, if you will, for they do not have life.

Lazarus Was the Garbage Can at Dives' Gate

In the East, when the food was eaten, one's bread was used to wipe the hands off. It was this bread that Lazarus was being given. He was getting a handout, but he was not being given a hand.

How often the church of which I am a part, as an institution, only gives handouts. We become concerned about people at Christmas (baskets, toys), Thanksgiving, and revival time. We do not have a perennial concern about their welfare. It comes only in a flash, only in a moment, only in seasons.

We get a little disturbed at Home Missions Week or Lottie Moon time or some special emphasis. But too often the church gives handouts when people really need hands of encouragement and help.

Your Lazarus

My main purpose is simply to ask you, "What about the Lazarus at your gate? That Lazarus is lost—lost from people, from personhood, from joy. He can't find his way to God. He needs you to direct him. He needs you to show him the way. That Lazarus may be a child; he may be an adult; he may be in your church; he may be living next door to the church; but he is, in a sense, every man who is in need, who does not know Jesus Christ, or who needs to be taught the ways of Jesus Christ.

I am afraid so often we read this story and say, "You know, that old rich man should have done better toward Lazarus. He should have been more compassionate. He should have gotten with it."

And I am afraid sometimes that we leave this story the same way the rich man did. We still have not been moved by the Lazarus at our gate. We still have not heard the cries of humanity at our door. We still leave our Lazarus to starve.

Organized Religion

I believe that Jesus was putting his finger on organized religion in this story. I think he was using the rich man as a typical example of Judaism. Judaism was rich. Judaism had the bread. Judaism had the spiritual garments, but she wrapped those garments around her, she clutched the bread and she kept her riches, she did not share, she did not open the door, she forgot the Gentiles and the Samaritans.

Do you hear the cries of your brother? Will the church stay behind her stained glass windows and sing her hymns while the multitudes are starving at her doors for wholeness, for a celebration of life, for personhood, for purpose, for redemptive relationships?

The question that all of us must answer is a question that the whole church is concerned with—bringing men to life in Jesus Christ, teaching those men the life-style of the Christian pilgrimage.

WHO ARE WE?

Pillars of the congregation.
In the same pew Sunday by Sunday:
Nodding assent to sermons that please,
Nodding "hello" to men by the door.
With the conventional nods,
    we come and we go—
a nod and a habit and sad self-delusion,
    Good God, forbid! Make us more aware.

Lead us to . . .
    The mechanized man in his mechanized job,
    The illiterate woman in a literate world,
    The rejected child on a crumbling stoop,
    The purposeless teenager, consumed by quiet
      terror.
    Lead us from the comfort of the sanctuary—
    Where thy strength can make us stronger—
    Into the crowd, into the lonely places,
    Where the gospel of love can make men
      whole.

WHO ARE WE?
We are the church.

AND WHERE IS THE CHURCH?
May we be scattered about in the world,
Armed with a miracle: God's love in action!

—Sheilia Campbell

Your Lazarus is waiting!

9.
Not Our Kind of Folks

J. Clark Hensley

"Treat 'em right, but they are not our kind of folks," Mother said.

"What do you mean?" I wanted to know.

"You'll see," she replied.

We played with those neighbor children. They cheated. We were taught to be kind. They stole. We were taught to respect property rights. They used vulgarity and profanity. We were scolded for using slang and avoided profanity. They would seek to settle arguments by bullying with fists or a stick. Though we sometimes lost our tempers and fought momentarily, we were taught this was the wrong way to settle differences. Indeed, in a rural setting with little economic differences, I felt the cultural gap. They were *not* our kind of folks.

Who Are Patriots?

"Come see the yellow star they have put up for _____!" It was during World War I. The yellow star was for a "conscientious objector." It was on the flag in the church where other stars were placed for men in the service. A brilliant gold star designated a man killed in action and he was buried in a neighboring cemetery with a monument topped by a soldier with a gun. Later, a black star was added to the flag indicating a deserter. Hearing an emotional conversation, I became quite upset about one who would let his country down by being a conscientious objector or by deserting. Yet my heart was filled with anxiety when my father was called before the draft board and my mother said, "He may have to go." Imagine our joy when Dad returned with a deferment because he was a farmer with four children. There was no stigma to a deferment.

Politics, Too!

"He's a black Republican," Mother said. There is something bad about being a Republican, I thought. It had no reference to race or history. Mother's people were Democrats and her grandparents had been robbed by bushwhackers whom they thought were Union sympathizers. Though the Hensleys were traditional Democrats, Grandma Hensley was a Republican. When women's suffrage came in, she voted Republican and canceled Grandpa's Democratic vote. Issues were not too significant to my people, only parties. Once I made the mistake of confiding that I had voted for some Republicans. Forgiveness was long coming and we never discussed national politics after that, only the local political contests.

Care of Aged

My first introduction to the Ku Klux Klan was the appearance of a group in a local Methodist church one Sunday night. They presented the pastor with a gift of fifty dollars in cash, a lot of money then, and left. I never knew why the gift was given. For good will, I suppose. Later my dad asked me to help him build a huge cross, wrap it with gunny sacks, and haul it to a high ridge on our own property, but next to a neighbor's. Dad said it was for the neighbor's benefit as we burned it that night. There were a few other neighbors present. They were incensed because the first neighbor mentioned had his mother deed him her farm on the condition that he would care for her the remainder of her life (she was already in her late eighties) and then, because of her senility, he had her committed to the "county farm." I recall that my grandparents told him they would prefer he go elsewhere for his merchandise and that the neighbors refused to trade livestock or share tools. This prejudice on the basis of practices, with the attendant isolation, had a profound effect on me in terms of respect and responsibility in the treatment of the aged. In contrast, I felt so intensely the love of parents, grandparents, and a great-grandmother. I was puzzled by what I perceived to be extreme cruelty on the part of a son toward his mother.

Religion

Along the way I became very prejudiced against
Catholics. There were few in the county and they
lived fifteen or twenty miles away. But they wor-
shiped Mary and the Pope. They used a foreign
language. There was a lot of secrecy about their
religion. I heard many tales; I don't remember from
whom. I never saw a priest, a nun, or a person I
knew was a Catholic! But they were all neatly filed
away in my mind's computer and certainly were
not my kind of folks.

Big Business

But one of the worst "not my kinds" was the chain
produce house, later called the chain grocery store.
They could outbid my grandparents for chickens,
eggs, and cream and could undersell them on com-
modities. For years Grandpa operated a country
store which was actually a small department store.
His prices were legitimate. He extended credit lib-
erally. He took the bankrupt law once and went
broke the second time because of his generosity and
tenderheartedness. He could not turn people down,
especially if they sent their children to the store
for something. But when the chains came in, we
heard from Grandma, who had fire in her eye and
anger in her voice. People who owed Grandpa would
drive twelve to fifteen miles to save an extra penny
per dozen eggs, a penny on a pound of sugar or
five cents on a sack of flour, and then perhaps stop

back by Grandpa's store to buy on credit. It didn't occur to Grandma to blame the people. She "cussed" the chain stores. And, as a little boy, I didn't like them either! They sure weren't "our kind of folks." I find it tempting today to transfer this feeling in the case of the little man versus big business.

Divorced!

After a few days of my first year of school, my heart was broken. I was told, "You don't belong to your daddy. Your father is _____." The blank is not used for privacy; I have actually forgotten the name. Naturally, I went to Mother. I still remember the painful expression on her face, but I can also feel the comfort of her arms as she quietly said, "Yes, Clark, you belong to Daddy. He is your father. We were married in August, 1911, and you were born June 16, 1912. It takes nine months for a baby to be born. Now let's count it up and see how long after we were married you were born." Then she went on to say, "Since this has come up, and so that you will understand, I need to tell you that I was married to _____. But he was very mean to me. He beat me so much he almost killed me, and finally Pa told me I just had to leave him for surely God didn't want me to live with a man who was so mean and cruel. So, I divorced him."

"What does divorce mean?" I asked.

"That we are not married anymore," Mother answered.

Then she continued, "After a few years, I met

your dad. We loved each other and were married. We wanted to have a family, and you are our first-born. We have you because we wanted you and love you. Now we have your two brothers. You are all ours, and we love you all." My mother kissed me, hugged me close to her a few moments, relaxed her arms and said, "So if anyone tells you again that you are not Daddy's boy, tell them you asked your mother and she said that this is not so, that you do belong to Daddy, and your mother ought to know."

The matter was never mentioned again. But a few things came through, loud and clear. For some reason, it was a terrible thing to be divorced. People talked about you. But I felt so much tenderness and compassion toward my mother who had endured such cruelty. That was worse than divorce, it seemed to me. Then I keenly felt her recognition that her past mistake was causing me pain and sensed the trauma she was undergoing in sharing with me what she thought I had to know to clear up my own grief. I can remember, too, a feeling of contempt for those who had wounded us both by gossiping about Mother and raising questions about me. Somehow I sensed that Mother felt she had done something terribly wrong and "her sin was being visited upon her child." Yet it was Mother who had taught us to forgive, to turn the other cheek, to be kind to each other, to love one another, and especially that God loves us all. She, more than anyone I knew as a child, was a mediator of God's love and grace. I didn't understand the concept then, but I knew the feeling. Divorce must have been very difficult in the early 1900's. The stigma must have been almost unbearable. I became a victim of the vicious prejudice in 1918. But those who gossiped about my mother were not my kind of folks.

Alcoholics

My father drank socially, that is, with anyone he associated with who drank, and he was frequently drunk. Fortunately, he was never abusive with his family and would come home seeming somewhat ashamed, or at least embarrassed. No doubt he must have promised Mother often he would not drink again. Though she never nagged him, she was always hurt and disappointed. But the addictive effect of this depressant drug took its toll. We all worried about his safety and health. Eventually, we were concerned about our financial security and bread on the table. Dad was a trader as well as a farmer. The hired help kept the farm work going and Dad kept himself going. He was honest, a good judge of livestock, and could make money handily when his judgment was not befuddled by alcohol, either beer or whiskey. My hostility against the bottle, against my dad, against anyone who drank, became greater as time passed. One day the country doctor arrived on horseback to see my sick mother and left his bottle on the back porch. This was too much. I poured out the liquor and broke the bottle near his horse's feet. Dad gave me a hard whipping, which I deserved for a violation of property rights. But this only added to my hostility toward liquor and those who drank.

During the prohibition era my dad became a "recovered alcoholic." Since his supply dried up, he dried out. Many did! Contrary to what the moderationists and liquor industry people say about prohibition being a failure, it was a huge success as far as our family was concerned.

As a teenage boy, I made many speeches for the abstinence and prohibition cause. On one occasion, a cousin became very angry and caught me outside the church to say, "Clark, you ought to be ashamed to talk like that, knowing how your dad drinks." I replied, "That is the main reason I am against liquor so much. I know what it has done to our family, and especially to one whom I love." I surely felt that those who profiteered on the weaknesses of others through beverage alcohol were not my kind of folks.

By the grace of God I have learned to sit with an alcoholic without judgment. My own neighbor-love reaches out to the person and the family. I may be called upon to offer *tough* love—to lead the alcoholic to accept or feel responsibility for his own actions and not allow him to evade, avoid, scapegoat, or cop out. Probably more than for any other reason, since I suffered with my father in his drinking and recovery, I can say, "These are my kind of folks."

Against Educated Ministry

"Anyone as smart as you are ought to go to high

school," my teacher said. My folks wanted me to have more education, but there didn't seem to be a way. There was no bus transportation then and tuition for nonresident students was fifty dollars per year. I thought, "What's the use? I don't need an education. I'm going to be a preacher and maybe an auctioneer, too, and you don't need an education to be either one." At least that is what a preacher said in a revival meeting down at Leffler. "You just follow the Holy Spirit," he said. "These educated preachers are all 'modernists' and they don't believe the Bible is true." I didn't know what a modernist was, but it sounded bad. "If you are called to preach, just preach the word of God. Just tell people what comes into your mind by the Holy Spirit." He didn't know, or forgot to say, that there are other ways one can get a thought except by the Holy Spirit. So educated preachers weren't my kind, either. I knew that man was Spirit-filled; he said he was. Besides, there were people who got excited and praised God aloud. A woman preacher danced for joy and several people uttered strange sounds. They called it "speaking in tongues." They said, "If you get the Spirit you can do it, too." So educated preachers weren't for me. The evidence was right there. You didn't need an education if you were going to be a preacher.

Blacks!

Mr. and Mrs. Jeff Lightfoot and her parents rented a farm in our community. The Lightfoots were black. I recall that Grandma wondered if some of the

customers would stop trading with them if the
Lightfoots were sold what they needed. But it
seemed only a passing thought. There must not have
been too much consternation for the four of them
united with the Methodist church, and soon Mrs.
Lightfood was the pianist and the other three were
singing in the choir. They visited with us frequently.
Mr. Lightfoot had a most contagious laugh. He was
fun to be around. As far as I was concerned, he
was like others except for color, and this soon faded
with familiarity. At watermelon season time, the
Lightfoots invited the whole neighborhood for a
cutting. Everybody went. Perhaps there was safety
in numbers. I really don't think they were fully
accepted. After a few years they decided to sell out
and move to the county seat town. On the day of
the sale, my mother realized that the Lightfoot
family would need a place to sleep that night and
I remember her saying, "I don't care what some
of the neighbors may say, I am going to ask them
to spend the night." And she did, including supper
and breakfast. I also recall she had the washing on
the line soon after they left. Remembering that
bathing and sanitary facilities were quite primitive
then, I must say in all fairness to my Christian
mother that she would have done the same thing
had the company been our kind of folks.

Haves Versus Have-Nots

Really, we knew little about rich and poor ways.
We were all below the poverty level, but no one

ever told us. We were quite self-sufficient in raising our own food. A few staples had to be purchased along with shoes for winter and changes of clothing. Our basic needs were met. We were really unaware that some others had much more. So the "haves" and "have-nots" did not enter the portals of prejudice at that time.

These differences were soon brought into focus. Being encouraged by my school teacher and the Sunday School superintendent, who put me in touch with his brother, I looked into the possibility of going on to high school. The brother was the janitor at the school and was permitted to select one boy to help with the work in return for free tuition. While blue denim overalls were acceptable school attire, a number of the young men wore shirt and trouser combinations and most seemed to have one dress suit. They also had spending money. A few earned it, but most had an allowance. To go to the soda fountain after school was the in thing. I was spared this because of my sweeping job at the school, but there were other times, like after the game and after church and Saturday afternoon. The "haves" had it better than the "have-nots."

I did my own cooking in my room. My parents managed two dollars and fifty cents per week for all grocery expenses and paid my room rent. The second year I was on my own financially and had to borrow. By the senior year, my parents moved into a consolidated school district where tuition was free. I walked five miles each way and was excused from physical education. Some had horses to ride.

A few had cars to drive. The "haves" had it better than the "have-nots."

During high school years, I began to feel the tension between labor and management. People lost jobs as the crash came. The Great Depression followed. Some who had been "haves" were now the "have-nots" and they had the most difficult adjustment. With radio and better forms of communication, I was more aware of what was going on and felt keenly for those in the soup lines of the great cities and especially for their little children. I had experienced the comforts of indoor plumbing and the luxury of a bathtub. I knew the joys of the telephone, train ride, the truck, and the Model T. I didn't want to go back to kerosene lights. Yet being identified with rural people, I sensed prejudice toward the city. Even now, in many ways, the people of rural backgrounds are my kind of folks.

Enlarged Vision

In my first pastorates, a few educated people encouraged me to go to college. This encouragement finally took the form of a consolidated debt loan of two hundred dollars enabling me to take the giant step. My sights had been raised to junior college achievement, but I did not stop until the A.B. work was completed. With seminary now as a goal, I had conquered my prejudice against an educated ministry. After finally earning a doctorate, the only educational prejudice I have is toward the cheap degrees so many seek today as status symbols.

College and seminary not only lifted my horizons and broadened my sympathies academically, but gave me opportunities for personal relationships with Japanese, Mexicans, Africans, South Americans, and peoples of European nations. My first experience with the American Indian occurred during this time, and it was not until twenty years later that I learned there were still those prejudiced against the Indian. I had thought we ought to be grateful for their relinquishing this wonderful country so we could have freedom. During these years of study, I learned something of the tensions between so many people and felt I had a smattering of intellectual understanding as to some of the contributing factors. It was while researching material for the book *My Father Is Rich* that I learned of the extreme prejudice of many Indians toward the paleface. This is readily understood when you feel the pathos and injustice of the Trail of Tears.

Labor-Management

The labor-management prejudices were highlighted during my first pastorate out of college. Located in a suburban section composed of factory laborers, I often found myself in the middle of labor disputes, though management never knew they had a friend (or enemy), as the situation seemed to demand. With the slowly rising economy, wages lagged and grievances were common. Both the union business representative and president of the union were members of our church, as were some committee members. Many strategy sessions were held in my office. Constantly, I felt the prejudicial feelings of the laborers as reflected by these men. I tried to help them be more objective, but some of the attitudes rubbed off. I learned the advantages and the usual necessity of collective bargaining. I always maintained that a worker ought to have a right to work without being coerced to join a union. The men, along with me, were opposed to violent tactics, though the right to strike was maintained. We found that reasonable arbitration could usually accomplish their purposes and while the threat of a strike was there, it was to be used as a last resort. During my eight years of counseling it was never used. Five years later a strike was called, unreasonable demands were made, and the company closed the factory and moved away.

I have never been so involved since, though I have been a counselor at times for both management and laborer. As many do, I now feel the tensions more as they affect me personally, such as a deprivation of services I feel I have a right to expect. However, I believe I am experientially equipped to empathize with both labor and management when disputes arise, if they are close enough to me for an adequate understanding of the issues. Either can be my kind of folks.

Some Good Friends Have Money

In the meantime I have known many people of wealth and have learned that money and character can mix well. The "haves" are often generous, community and/or church minded persons who rejoice in giving to make possible a better life for the "have-nots." I have seen much compassion and concern for others among the "haves." I have found more covetousness among the "have-nots." "Haves" more often love people and use things while "have-nots" are tempted to love things and use people. I am no longer prejudiced toward persons of wealth, nor am I in awe of them. They, too, are people for whom Christ died. They can be tough and tender, lonely and frightened, shunned and ridiculed, misunderstood and maligned, lovable and lovely. Several of our best friends are among the "haves" and are definitely our kind of folks.

Coping with Religious Prejudice

Finally, I was really exposed to Catholicism. Edgar made a profession of faith. On the night he was to be baptized, I found a basket of beautiful mums at the church. The attached note read, "Give one of these to each person being baptized and keep the rest for yourself." When I went to the local florist, who employed Edgar, to thank her for the flowers, she remarked about the beauty and significance of the baptism. She was a Catholic. Though our views on baptism were different, I felt that she was not far from the kingdom.

Later, I had Catholic neighbors. They were among the best I have ever had. Still later, our church was next to the Catholic church, and I found them to

be good neighbors, too. Personal acquaintances with
priests have ripened into friendships. When Bernard
Law of Mississippi was appointed bishop of a diocese
in Missouri, I could write him a sincere word of
concern and assurance of my prayers. Though I do
not accept some of the theology or some of the
ethical and political concepts of the Catholic
Church, I find myself feeling that many of my Catholic friends are my kind of folks. A few years ago
I wondered why I was once so prejudiced against
the Catholics. The only reason I could find was that
I didn't really know them.

Peacemakers

I am still prejudiced toward our nation. The flag
is the most beautiful piece of cloth in the world
to me. One who travels abroad always feels relieved
to get back to the United States for a breath of freer
air. I am more critical of our history and of our
leadership as statesmen degenerate to mere politicians. I do not think politics is dirty, but some dirty
people get into politics. I still believe the system
can be improved from within. I believe in citizen-
ship involvement. I pray for our elected leaders and
seek to influence their views toward what I believe
to be right. I know what it is to have my life and
position threatened because I publicly espoused
clean government. It is not pleasant to live in fear
of being bombed, shot, or having members of my
family hurt. And this did not happen in Mississippi!
So from the time I heard the terrifying tales of

the terrible Germans from our hired man, who served in World War I; to a week spent in Washington D.C. considering the plight of the conscientious objector; I have come from "my country, right or wrong" to the concept of "when wrong, make her right and when right, support her in right." I have moved from aggressive militancy to the position that peacemakers and peacekeepers are my kind of folks.

Black-White Pilgrimage

Let us continue to follow the racial strand of my pilgrimage as it affects black and white relationships. In college I taught church leadership courses in black churches. In Moberly, Missouri, the only pastor at that time with an earned doctor's degree was a black man. On his sixteenth anniversary with the church, the newspaper carried a story complimentary to his community and church leadership.

This pastor and I exchanged pulpits and choirs from time to time. We worked together in Vacation Bible School leadership training. Integration of churches never occurred to us in the mid-thirties. Dialogue; appreciation; counsel; combined ministers meetings made up the acceptable pattern. The same was true in Kansas City and later in Nashville and Pulaski, Tennessee. Today such a pattern of fraternalism would be called paternalism or Uncle Tom religion. But our motives were pure then. We were different in color and culture, but one was not better than the other. Each had his place to fill.

I served on the board of the Urban League in

Kansas City in the early forties. We met at the black YMCA or at one of the Negro churches. Our primary task was to study housing trends and recommend zoning ordinances to the city fathers. The population pressures often resulted in the overrunning of former white neighborhoods by the blacks. But the segregation was called de facto. We did not deal with other ethnic groups that clustered in various areas of the city.

In Nashville I had the privilege of serving as a volunteer chaplain in the newly purchased Baptist Hospital and ministered to some in the black ward. In Pulaski, a black physician was admitted to hospital practice. I was told by my physician to call Dr. Spotts, the black man, without a moment's hesitation, should I have need for a doctor when he was not available.

Pulaski, Tennessee—that's another story! A typical Southern town in population make-up. Often, as people would move in, I would be told, "Pastor, they are not our kind of folks." But a lot of wonderful, dedicated Christlike people live there. Upon our arrival, the Methodist preacher knelt in our living room and prayed for our ministry. A Jewish merchant sent a Christmas present. These two acts were symbolic of the spirit of so many. The Ku Klux Klan was organized there on December 24, 1865, as a boredom-release fun experience. The power it would have for fear or intimidation was later discovered only by accident. None of the original founders in their wildest dreams would have thought of such repressive activity as is described in Don

Whitehead's *Attack on Terror: The FBI Against the Ku Klux Klan in Mississippi,* published in 1970 by Funk and Wagnalls.

In the early fifties we followed the pattern of an integrated ministerial association, Good Friday and Easter observances and Vacation Bible School activities. I feel that the relationship between the church people contributed to the fact that the Pulaski, Tennessee, school system was completely integrated without a court order, as were swimming pool and park facilities.

The tension building in the South following the Brown decision did not seem to alarm Pulaskians. Some of the black community feared that if school integration was precipitated too hastily, they would lose their jobs and the white community feared the loss of strong black leadership. It was during this period of uncertainty about the future that I received a call from Brother Howard, the longtime pastor of a black Baptist church. He wanted to see me immediately. The matter was urgent. I built up considerable apprehension and anxiety as I waited for our four o'clock appointment. Was there some incident of which I was not aware?

Four o'clock. Brother Howard and I exchanged greetings. He seated himself, crossed his legs, cleared his throat, shifted his position, and recrossed his legs. I waited. "Doctor," he began, "I just had an impression of the Holy Spirit that I should come down here and tell you what a leavening influence you are in our community." He continued, "Many of our people worship with you by means of radio.

They listen to your morning devotional broadcasts. They believe in you and your church people. They are being helped by your ministry. They are constantly sharing with me the strength and support they feel. Now, Doctor, I would like to pray again with you for all our people, black and white." So we knelt and prayed together as we had frequently done and as heaven came down I thought of the lines of the old hymn, "There is a calm, a sure retreat; 'Tis found beneath the mercy seat."

And the Jewish People . . .

Pulaski also has a group of Jewish families, some of whom became our very good friends. Each season it was my privilege to send them Hanukkah greetings and it is our joy to receive annual greetings at Christmastime with the significant shalom.

One of my Jewish friends told me, "We always listen to you preach and when our friends from Nashville come down and eleven o'clock comes, we say, "Gather by the radio. We always listen to the First Baptist Church services." Then he said, "You know what I like about your preaching? Well, perhaps it is not your preaching. It's the praying. When you are talking with our heavenly Father, I just feel you are reaching out and including me, too."

The main reason for relating these incidents is to say that when a church congregation mediates God's love and grace in practical, visible ways, the community feels and responds to it. Surely these were our kind of folks.

In 1958, I became director of missions in Jackson, Mississippi. The Hinds Baptist Association since 1952 has sponsored the Hart Baptist Center, named for the founder and first director, Gertrude T. Hart. All the workers have always been black. The center has had capacity enrollment almost from the beginning. Upon my arrival to inspect the temporary rented quarters, two children had to move out to give me room to stand as they were all packed into an assembly room. In 1960, with the help of the Annie Armstrong Easter offering, a modern building was erected to give opportunity for a more adequate nursery and day care facility. Never during the time of the Freedom Riders, marches, the sit-ins, and other efforts to break segregation barriers did I feel it dangerous to go into this area, day or night.

On the way to my office one morning, I heard a radio newsman in New York say, "It is not safe in Jackson, Mississippi, for a black person to be on the street this morning." As I drove along, there were blacks everywhere, either driving or walking nonchalantly. I said to myself, "I guess they haven't heard the news." About 9:30 that morning Miss Hart came to see the bookkeeper, as was her custom. I said in mock alarm, "Miss Hart, what are you doing here? Don't you know it is not safe for a black person to be on the street this morning?" "Who said so?" she asked, her eyes flashing. "A newsman in New York," I replied. "Phooey on him!" was her answer.

The tension was sometimes high and there were incidents. Some were real. Some were contrived by

the news media. All were sad and serious. Black
and white Christian leaders are still working together in Christian love trying to solve these problems. In my opinion, those of both races who have
worked through the Mississippi Baptist Seminary
(through twenty-eight extension centers, the seminary has trained black ministerial and lay church
leaders since 1944) program, all over the state, have
done much to promote understanding and goodwill.
They are my kind of folks.

No Color Lines

In 1966 when I became executive director of the
Christian Action Commission, I was asked about the
commission and race. "We are colorless," I replied.
While we were commissioned as an educational and
resource agency for Mississippi Baptists and Mississippi Baptist churches, we have always made all
of our materials and resources available for all Mississippi citizens.

Human Relations

Our policy statement concerning human relations
reads as follows:

"Human relations is at the center of God's purpose
for His universe and His people. God created a good
world that functioned in harmony, but man rebelled
and did not function as God intended. The result
was his alienation from God and his fellowman. Man
was then confronted with a hostile world; he became

insecure, greedy, and anxious. When a man does not know who his father is, he does not know who his brother is. God was not content to leave people in an alienated state but is working toward bringing all men together through reconciliation with Himself.

"In human relations we seek to develop an understanding of alienation and help restore communication and reconciliation whether the barriers be economic, cultural, intellectual, social, racial, creedal, or spiritual. Because of the multifaceted nature of alienation, the techniques for achieving better human relations must be developed in each community situation. The Christian Action Commission will seek to discover and suggest resources to cope with problems that face churches in these areas. We recognize that often the Gospel does more than "get people saved" as the power of God moves one to become a Christian in his life-style. The reconciled then become reconcilers and the kind of human relations God intended becomes possible.

"One important task is to break down barriers which separate us and deny rights and opportunities to some. This can best be done by building lines of communication that we might open doors of understanding and bridge the gaps between economic classes, cultural and ethnic groups, the educated and the illiterate, as well as develop an understanding of other religious practices. This can be done without the loss of evangelical zeal or sense of mission.

"Some areas of concern may be poverty, housing

problems, employer-employee relationships, community health conditions, welfare standards and problems, educational opportunities for the underprivileged, relationships between law enforcement groups and the community, and community recreational facilities for all, youth to the aged."

Trying to Avoid Prejudice in Children

In 1965 we took our boys to the Baptist World Alliance in Miami Beach. We wanted them to be in an international atmosphere and experience some fellowship with black people who were well mannered, and spiritually motivated. They were very impressed with the blacks they met. We made much of the sermon by Dr. Jackson, longtime black pastor in Chicago, and especially of the inspirational highlight for us when Dr. H. H. Hobbs congratulated the newly-elected black president from Liberia by saying, "I shake hands with my friends; those whom I love I embrace." Whereupon he gave Dr. Tolbert a kiss on the cheek.

However, the hotel we stayed in housed people mostly from the Bronx. Those Jews were loud, uncouth, vulgar, and rude. As we drove out of Miami the boys were really evidencing prejudice toward the Jews. We reiterated our desire that the Alliance would contribute to less racial prejudice rather than more. We reminded them of their playmates in Pulaski who were Jewish and what fine people they were. They then decided that, after all, these were our kind of folks.

Help for Divorced

In our culture perhaps one of the most serious and damaging prejudices so widely held is against divorced persons. In many churches they are shunned or ignored. They wear the stigma of a marriage failure. One may fail in anything else, but not this. Not to the extent that he gets a legal divorce. There is little concern for the affectional divorce that always precedes the legal divorce. It is not considered that a legal divorce may be the only decent way to bury a dead marriage. Not much attention, if any, is given to the church's failure in preparation for marriage, in premarital counseling or failure to give supportive help in the adjustment years. The divorced person cannot be a Sunday School teacher, certainly not a deacon. A man never married can sow his wild oats, be sexually promiscuous, a dope addict, then join the church and be ordained to the ministry and become an evangelist, titillating his audience with his life's story. But to be divorced seems to some, the unpardonable sin. Someone has said the army of the Lord is the only place where other soldiers will shoot their own wounded.

Some would allow for divorce, but not for remarriage. All sorts of judgment statements are made as people play God. Preachers have sometimes aided this prejudicial attitude by preaching legalism instead of grace. People, including preachers, often adjust their attitude and sometimes their Scripture interpretation when divorce affects someone in their family. Several chapters could be written of those who have softened their attitudes and pulpit expressions after a son or daughter obtained a divorce.

Make no mistake about it. Divorce is a sin. But it is not the unpardonable sin. When God forgives sin, the Bible says, "He remembers it against us no more." Being justified freely by his grace through the redemption in Christ Jesus means that in God's sight it is just as if we had not sinned. Calvary covers it all! We do not have complete atonement for all those who have married and stayed that way (though some have lived in a hell on earth) and a limited atonement for the divorced person that would say "Christ can cleanse you from all sin except this." In the New Testament we learn that Jesus' response to failure, all kinds of failure, was conditioned by grace. He epitomized the royal law of love and demonstrated how much God so loves!

I am able to overcome any tendency to prejudice toward the divorced person because I, too, have failed and in so many ways. But I know God's grace in response to my failures, to my missing the mark, to my falling short. Thus persons who have suffered divorce are my kind of folks.

I have discussed various areas of prejudice encountered in my own make-up and experience: culture, patriotic expression, politics, care for aged, religion, big business vs. the little man, divorce stigma in the community, the alcoholic and problem drinker, opposition to an educated ministry, early community acceptance of blacks, haves vs. have-nots, rural vs. urban, other ethnic groups, labor and management, toward nationalism, black and white relations, Jew and non-Jew, toward divorced persons in church groups.

Expressions of Prejudice

I have observed that prejudice is an opinion formed about a person or a group of persons before enough facts have been gathered to make a valid judgment. One may also be prejudiced to issues. Once prejudice is formed, it is very difficult to eliminate. Often people try to find Scriptures or illustrations to back up their feelings and attitudes.

We express prejudice by attitude when we feel better by looking down on someone or by feeling contempt for them. We may show it by language used when we talk about another—not only in what is said but by nonverbal methods of body language and voice inflection. We may discriminate in our behavior toward a person and thus express our prejudice.

What harm is prejudice?

1. It harms the person who is prejudiced. When we tend to act without thinking or on the basis of prejudging, we also tend not to be as Christian as we should.

2. Prejudice creates resentment, inferior feelings, desire for revenge, and sometimes hopelessness.

3. Some forms of prejudice as practiced by church groups may harm or nullify the Christian witness in the community as well as hinder our representatives who work in the mission fields in our

behalf.

4. As citizen groups express prejudice, they harm our national image with other groups, handicap understanding and hinder efforts toward peaceful relationships.

Antidotes for Prejudice

How can we cope with prejudice? We must recognize it as basically a moral and spiritual problem. We cannot deal with it adequately by laws, force, political or economic measures. As Christians we must seek to have the mind of Christ, letting him shape our attitudes and control our actions.

I recommend the method I have used in this treatise, namely to try to identify personal prejudices, sort them out, get at the facts as best we can. Becoming acquainted with people from other groups often reveals that our opinions and fears are ill founded.

For whatever it may be worth, I have learned some helpful mental attitudes to deal with prejudice formation. They may be called antidotes for prejudice, considering that prejudice is spiritual poison.

1. Suspend judgment. Do not allow first impressions to unduly influence you. If I feel that I do not like a person, I ask not, "What is it in him that I do not like?" but rather, "What is it in me that causes me to dislike him?" Do I project former prejudices or hostilities or guilt feelings on him? After seeing him in a number of circumstances I can better form an opinion as to the relationship

I may desire with him. At least I can be more objective.

2. Avoid stereotyping. I must be careful about thinking, "All _____ are like that." "Everybody knows. . . ." "The British don't have a sense of humor." "All Jews are after your money." "All Episcopalians are social drinkers." "All divorced persons want to remarry and are on the prowl." "Most church members are hypocrites." "You can't trust deacons." "All preachers talk about is money." "All politicians are crooked." "All lawyers lie." "Doctors don't care about you as a person."

3. Accept people as they are. I don't have to approve of their values or practices to believe in their inherent worth, to learn from them, or to respect the dignity of their personhood.

4. Try to get in their skin. Try to feel their perspective. I ask myself, "Given their background, would I react the same?" The book *Black Like Me* by Griffen helped me feel a minority race view.

5. Appreciate your own uniqueness and background, but don't be hidebound, tradition-bound, intellectually rutty or religiously nutty. Accept and love yourself. Seek to mature spiritually, and love others and God unconditionally.

6. Learn to live with differences such as color, culture, religious beliefs, political ideology. This does not mean that I am to stifle my personal convictions.

I am convinced that those who are not our kind of folks may become our kind of folks as we recognize our brothers and sisters in the family of God.

10.
Changing Mirrors Into Windows

Dick Brogan

(*Acts 4:32*).

History says that there was a king who did a very strange thing. He took all of the windows out of his palace and hung mirrors in their place. Then he could sit at his royal banquet tables, dressed in his regal robes, assuming the rest of the world looked like he looked and had the same needs he had. The tragedy of this story was that outside those mirrors were people who were hungry and needed companionship. But he lived to himself, for himself, and died by himself.

That man did something that we often do as individuals. We are guilty of mirror worship. But the church in Acts did just the opposite. They turned their mirrors into windows.

Listen! Acts 4:32 says, "All of the believers were of one heart and mind, and no one felt that what he owned was his own; everyone was sharing" (TLB).

Let me share my own personal pilgrimage in moving my life from the mirror mentality toward the window concept. Most of us stay in front of the mirror too long in our own lives. I'm glad that I had a mirror to look into today. I've tried to rearrange what has been given me. Some do a better job than others!

But what I want to suggest to you is that it is possible for a person to go through life with only the mirror concept. Jesus warned us in his teachings about mirror worship. Let me share three examples of the Master Teacher.

A Mirror Man—the Rich Fool

Do you remember the story in the twelfth chapter of Luke of the building fool? He took a survey of what he had. He had too much. He was going to have to enlarge his barn in order to take care of what possessed him. If anybody had a mirror mentality, this man did. It was "my barns and my soul and my life and my family." He died with a deadly case of my-itis.

Jesus said in essence, "All that you lived for is no longer yours. Life comes to a sudden judgment and all that you have acquired, you're going to leave." Here was a person who lived his mirror mentality. The result was he died looking at himself—spending eternity alone.

Mirror Mentality

Jesus talked to us in the story of the rich man and Lazarus. Jesus was trying to get the listeners to be very careful that they didn't allow their lives to develop into a mirror mentality.

This individual was very wealthy. He had acquired this world's goods. He was poverty-stricken in spirit. He died in wall-to-wall self. He refused to look outside of the windows in God's world to see his Lazarus. And so often it is easy for us to stay inside of our own little confinements, concerned about me and my wife and our son, John. No more, us three, and that's all. That spells mirror. That spells separation.

May I pinpoint for your attention the story of the good Samaritan. Jesus talked about life, the paths that lead in to all of us. Actually, the Jericho road reaches around the world. It's not just the road between Jerusalem and Jericho. It goes into every community and into every life. All of us face the kinds of decisions that the priest and Levite faced. They mirrored their religious traditions, passing by on the other side, leaving the man bruised, beaten, and alone. These actions indicated the priest and Levite were also guilty of mirror worship.

Look at your own life as I look at mine. Is it really possible to move away from mirror mentality? Is it really possible, is it conceivable, is there hope for any of us to move beyond mirror mentality as a way to think, as a life-style, as a philosophy, as a way to treat others? Is it within reason?

Jesus Was a Window Man!

Jesus Christ lived the window life! He was always actively caring about each person. When you read his life's story it seemed that he had the determination to do the Father's will! He was others centered in his existence. He was a neighbor regarder. He always looked at life not only from his own viewpoint but from his neighbor's perspective. He looked at life through his neighbor's eyes as well as his own. That's why we sing about him. That's one reason the Scripture came into existence. Jesus Christ had the unusual knack of living the window mentality, allowing himself to touch the lives of others. When you read his life you become paralyzed by his continual touching, healing, feeding, going out of himself toward those who are his brothers and kinfolk—humanity.

In my own life what has it meant to be a window person? I do not propose to be the ideal, nor have I arrived in being a window man. But that is certainly, as I understand the New Testament, the goal of every Christian. It is that goal for which we live. This is why we grow. This is why we worship! We study the Bible—to become window people, people through whom God's warmth and truth can be seen and channeled.

What about a window? A window serves to let light in. I often stand in my own home to allow the sunlight to fall on my body. It is something stimulating. The body is filled with zest when I stand and allow God's S-U-N to fall in upon my person. At various times in your own pilgrimage you have joined me—standing in awe as the S-O-N of God falls in upon your breast, into your mind, through your life.

I think that's what it means to be a window Christian, to allow God's Son-light to become a part of our existence. I think John said it well, "If we walk in the light He'll make a difference in what we become." (1 John 1:6, 7)

It lets the warmth of God's "Sun" (presence) in. Not only does a window allow the light to penetrate, it also allows the warmth of God's universe to permeate buildings that are cold and drab. I think in the near future we will heat and cool buildings by the use of the sun. Once we learn how to master it, once we learn how to control it, one day we will actually be heating and cooling buildings by a solar system. You can take a cold heart and allow God's Son to permeate his being and he will melt icy spirits. He'll put men together in church who nobody else would put together. He'll make the impossible seem like it should have been reality all along because he does isolate the "antiothers" germs of our souls. Pull back the curtain in your life and see yourself in "The Dance of the Dust." Through rays of the sun when one lives in the dark, he cannot see the dirt of his life.

Thank God for Windows!

A window lets you know what's happening in the world. I live on a very busy street. There seems to be something always happening in the front yard or in the street. Sometimes one of my children is in the street. That youngest one has stopped traffic for several blocks, so I go to the window often. I

hear noises, screams, and discussions between the
parents and children of our community. I go to the
window in my own house to find out what's happening!

Is the Church a Window?

The church of Jesus Christ must always have a
window outlook in God's world. God is doing something in his world. God is busy redeeming men.
God is infiltrating and interrupting man's activity.
God is pursuing man. God wants to be known, re-
vealing his will and person. We have been the dull
ones. So often we have been insensitive to know
where he's moving and what he's doing. The church
must be a window fellowship to be aware of what's
happening in God's universe.

Can You See Out of Your Church Windows?

I don't know how we arrived at the idea that
windows in churches should not be transparent. You
can't see out of most church windows. I don't think
that's a New Testament concept.

Symbolically, the church should always be able
to look beyond itself, to look at what God has done
and is doing in his world, to be able to see the hurts,
to be able to see the needs of the people wherever
they may be. In some of our churches we don't know
who is really hurting, even within our own congregation. We've lived this mirror existence so long
that we are not sensitive to those who are suffering

even within the body of Christ.

No Mirror Gazing

There is an interesting statement found in *No Longer Strangers*, by Bruce Larson, in which he describes the requirement of some young women who were in seminary. The candidate had to know how to cut and wash potatoes. Looking down the list of requirements, one of the things that caught my attention was that no member of this seminary class was allowed to look into the mirror more than three consecutive minutes at a time.

I wonder sometimes if God ought to blow the whistle on the church. Can you hear God saying to the twentieth-century assembly of Christians, "You've been looking in the mirror long enough. You've been so preoccupied with what takes place inside that you've forgotten that I work on the outside too." Maybe those who are perceptive should say, "Lord, we want to move beyond the mirror mentality to allow the church to be a window through which we can see God doing his redemptive work."

In 1 Corinthians 13, the apostle Paul does some unusual describing of the concept of Christian love. At the very end of that beautiful poem he says this: "It is like this: when I was a child I spoke and thought . . . as a child does. But when I became a man my thoughts grew far beyond those of my childhood and now I have put away the childish things. In the same way, we can see and understand

only a little about God now, as if we were peering
at his reflection in a poor mirror; but someday we
are going to see him in his completeness, face to
face" (vv. 11–12, TLB).

Move from the Mirror

Paul was saying to me, "Dick Brogan, in the
Christian pilgrimage you've got to learn to move
beyond the mirror." For you see, Christian love is
a window experience. Christian love keeps going
to the window relating to people in face-to-face
kinds of encounter.

The Difference in a Mirror and a Window

There's not really much difference between a
mirror and a window. All there is is a little mercury
and a little silver painted behind to make a mirror
reflect. You hold a mirror up to the sun and light
does not go through. It just reflects. You can't see
outside looking at a mirror.

What I think God is saying to me is, "If you'll
give me your life, Dick Brogan, it will be like a
mirror to begin with but I'll begin to scratch away
all of those ideas and evils that make you less than
you should be. I'll scratch away those subtle sins.
I'll help remove a lot of that selfishness and prejudice. I'll continually work with you, Dick Brogan,
if you'll allow me to take your life and slowly remove
that which makes your life a mirror. And I'll make
your life, if you'll let me have it, a window through

which men can see Jesus Christ, his grace, his strength."

Rights—Who Bestows Them

In every nation of this universe there is a new awakening to what constitutes the rights of a human being. Prejudice is one of the mental fences that keeps humanity from being free creatures. If I am continually looking into the mirror of my own rights, I may deny another fellow struggler some of his rights through me. We bestow rights and receive them. While one of my hands gives you a right, my other hand is receiving one from you.

Ponder these questions in light of your experience. Who is the giver of all rights? Is a person born with certain rights? If so, what are they? Does a person have to earn his rights? Is there a difference in civil rights and human rights? Does a Christian have rights that a non-Christian does not enjoy?

Of course, all of us must decide today how much of a mirror we are and how much we want God to make us a window. You can start the pilgrimage. It will be painful. It will require growth, a commitment to him who made you.

Who do you think you are? A window person? A mirror person?

About the Authors

RICHARD (DICK) BROGAN is director of Cooperative Ministries with National Baptists, Mississippi Baptist Convention Board. A native of Laurel, Mississippi, he is a graduate of Mississippi College and New Orleans Baptist Theological Seminary. Since 1963 he has participated in biracial gatherings as preacher, teacher, and conference leader. In 1971 the Mississippi Baptist Seminary honored him with the Doctor of Divinity "for his contribution to the betterment of mankind."

SAMUEL L. BOWMAN, also a Mississippi native, serves on the faculty of the Mississippi Baptist Seminary which bestowed on him a Doctor of Humanities in 1977. He has authored *Black Sons of Thunder*, a biographical study of twelve great black pulpiteers. He is president of the Baptist Ministers Union of Jackson, Mississippi. He is pastor of the Greater Clark Street Baptist Church in Jackson.

OWEN COOPER, a Mississippian, retired in 1973 as president of the Mississippi Chemical Corporation, Yazoo City, Mississippi. He is retired in name only. He has served as president of the Southern Baptist Convention and also president of the Mississippi Baptist Convention. Mr. Cooper has traveled extensively in fifty-nine foreign countries in the interest of Christian and humanitarian efforts. He is the author of *The Future Is Before Us*, a Broadman release.

J. CLARK HENSLEY hails from Missouri but has served in Mississippi for almost twenty years. He is the executive director of the Christian Action Commission, Mississippi Baptist Convention. Dr. Hensley received his doctorate from Midwestern Baptist Seminary, Kansas City, Missouri. He has been a pastor, seminary professor, and counselor. He has authored seven books, his latest, *Coping with Being Single Again*.

JAMES MILTON PORCH is pastor of the First Baptist Church, Tullahoma, Tennessee. From Morton, Mississippi, he is a graduate of Mississippi College and New Orleans Baptist Theological Seminary (M.Div. and Th.D.). He has led conferences at Ridgecrest and Glorieta and has contributed to numerous periodicals and publications. His last church in Mississippi was the Northside Baptist Church, Clinton.

ROBERT M. SHURDEN, a native of Greenville,

Mississippi, is assistant professor in the Division of Religion at Mississippi College. He is a graduate of Mississippi College and Southern Baptist Theological Seminary (M.Div. and Th.D.). He joined the MC staff in 1972.